CW00400824

Freedom

How To Live Your Life

For Jesus

Free From Anxiety About Money

Matt Bird

FOREWORD BY
Chuck Bentley

Copyright © 2019 Matt Bird

The moral right of the author has been asserted.

Apart from any fair dealing for the purposes of research or private study,
or criticism or review, as permitted under the Copyright, Designs and Patents
Act 1988, this publication may only be reproduced, stored or transmitted, in
any form or by any means, with the prior permission in writing of the
publishers, or in the case of reprographic reproduction in accordance with
the terms of licences issued by the Copyright Licensing Agency. Enquiries
concerning reproduction outside those terms should be sent to the publishers.

Matador
9 Priory Business Park,
Wistow Road, Kibworth Beauchamp,
Leicestershire. LE8 0RX
Tel: 0116 279 2299
Email: books@troubador.co.uk
Web: www.troubador.co.uk/matador
Twitter: @matadorbooks

ISBN 978 1789018 011
British Library Cataloguing in Publication Data.
A catalogue record for this book is available from the British Library.

Printed and bound in the UK by TJ International, Padstow, Cornwall
Typeset in 11pt Aldine by Troubador Publishing Ltd, Leicester, UK

Matador is an imprint of Troubador Publishing Ltd

MIX
Paper from
responsible sources
FSC® C013056

Kevin & Simone

Freedom

to live life for
Jesus!

Matt

Dedicated to my children Joseph, Matilda and Reuben.
I pray this book helps you live for Jesus free from anxiety
about money.

What People Say

"Matt's book is a powerful and practical solution to the problem of money that many people live with on a daily basis. It is easy to follow and full of biblical 'how to' wisdom that can transform your life!"
Pastor Agu, Irukwu, Senior Pastor of Jesus House

'Matt is an extraordinary communicator who speaks and writes from his heart and his head at the same time. Matt well understands relationships and this book will help you have a more healthy relationship with money. Matt speaks from a deep faith perspective and you will find that as he applies scripture to this topic (and helps us to do so as well) it results in Freedom!"
David Wills, President Emeritus of National Christian Foundation

"There's a reason why Jesus tells us so many times not to be anxious – he knows we all have the proclivity to be anxious! Matt's book offers practical advice on how we can find the financial contentment that Jesus so wants us to have in him."
Daryl Heald, Founder of Generosity Pathway

"Matt has done it again – quite an insightful, liberating and revolutionary book, presented in a language that is clear and easy to understand. The title could not be more apt."
Pastor Kingsley Appiagyei, Senior Pastor of Trinity Baptist Church

"Money can be a source of angst whether you have 'not enough' or 'too much'. That Jesus says more about money and possessions than heaven and hell means He knows it is a matter of the heart. Matt Bird nails it by combining scripture, principles, and personal examples. Read, contemplate, and be transformed!"
Bob Doll, Board Chair of Movement Day

"Freedom is a book that helps you deepen your faith in God as your provider while providing practical advice on how to use money as a tool to impact your family and the Kingdom. A recommended read to help you manage your treasure wisely and not let your treasure manage you."
Vince Birley, CEO of Vident Financial

"Matt Bird is an amazing power for good around the world, blending experience, charisma and Biblical wisdom as he comes alongside communities and businesses to help them bring about Heaven on Earth."
Henry Kaestner, Partner at Sovereigns Capital

"As I read this book, I couldn't stop thinking of friends, relatives, and others in my networks who I would love to recommend it to. It will help the reader get to the heart of what it is that makes people struggle with money and how to live a life of freedom in Jesus. More than that, this is a book rooted in the Bible and prayer and built on a strong Christian foundation."
Ram Gidoomal CBE, Chair of Stewardship

"This book is bold, biblical, practical and highly motivational. Matt Bird is a practitioner of what he preaches, and with this book is helping us not to be conformed to the ways of the current economic system that is producing an overwhelmingly broken culture. Apply the principles, and you will thrive and not just survive!"

Alan Platt,
Global leader of Doxa Deo / City Changers

"As someone who has spent a lifetime in an anxious state related to keeping an organization afloat, I was thrilled to see my friend Matt Bird address the subject so effectively. Jesus promises the possibility of a life free from financial anxiety, Matt gives ten very practical ways we can live that out."

Kevin Palau, President of Luis Palau Association

"Money is a great servant but a terrible master... and an even worse god! I pray that God will use this intensely practical and hope-filled book to set many free, release generosity, and help them discover a closer relationship with the God who gives us 'all things richly to enjoy'."

Paul Harcourt, National Leader of New Wine England

"Take the ten steps and find more than financial freedom. You will take hold of God's design for abundant living."

Dr. Gary G. Hoag, Generosity Monk

"It's refreshing to find a book that offers Biblical guidance about 'your walk' as a believer in Christ and growing financially in all things that our great God has to offer. A recommended read that could change your life!"

James McGovern, CEO of Charis Group Holdings

"*Matt Bird synthesises his personal experience, interviews, research and the Bible to give us ten highly practical steps that will lead to a personal action plan for financial freedom!*"
Tami Heim,
President/CEO of Christian Leadership Alliance

"*If you want to live in financial freedom, then getting your heart right and taking some practical steps are both absolutely crucial. Freedom has a great combination of biblical teaching and practical suggestions that will help you step into greater financial freedom in your life.*"
John Kirkby CBE,
Founder of Christians Against Poverty

"*Many of us worry about money but don't know what to do to break free from our anxiety. Freedom articulates simple principles and practices that we can adopt as we live thoughtful, faithful and generous lives for Jesus.*"
Tim Macready,
Chief Investment Officer of Christian Super

Contents

Foreword

It has been said that America and Britain are two nations divided by a common language.

My friend Matt Bird is British and uses words like *chuffed*, *skint* and *tosh*. I am an American and prefer different words with similar meaning like *pumped*, *broke* and *baloney*.

He says labour; I say labor.

He says that a written order for a bank to pay a specified amount from deposited funds is a cheque. Over here, we call it a check.

In spite of these nuanced differences, we Americans have many things in common with the Brits:

We both use money. It is a part of our daily lives.

We both need to know how to live our lives free from anxiety about money.

We both desire and need a pathway to financial freedom, whether we have lots of resources or very few.

Matt, who is both a business and non-profit leader, has written a candid account of his financial journey with insights and practical applications that he learned from experience and from the financial principles found in God's Word. It is a refreshing and inspiring account of how God has taught him what it means to be faithful and to strive for true riches.

As one who has walked a very similar path and cares deeply that Christians understand what Jesus says about this all-important topic of money, I am pleased to commend the work to you.

My own life was arrested by the words of Christ in Luke 16:10-11: "One who is faithful in a very little is also faithful in much, and one who is dishonest in a very little is also dishonest in much. If then you have not been faithful in the unrighteous wealth, who will entrust to you the true riches?" (ESV)

Jesus made two startling points crystal clear:

His standard with money is faithfulness, not success. I was struck (gobsmacked - as Matt might say) with the sobering reality that I was aiming at the wrong target! The first 40 years of my life had been oriented toward success in accumulating worldly wealth. I had no idea what it meant to be *faithful* with worldly wealth.

The promised reward for faithfulness with worldly wealth is *true riches*. Again, I was left void of any real knowledge of what Jesus was even talking about.

My life changed forever when I dedicated myself to knowing and applying what the Bible really says about managing money and becoming a faithful steward. Not only did I experience financial freedom, but also my life took on deeper meaning and purpose.

Matt and I both want you to know that Jesus came to set you free, to give you the ultimate reward of eternal, lasting riches. We hope this book will set you on the path toward abundant life with Jesus Christ at the centre.

As you work through the ten steps and exercises ahead, our desire is that you will grow as God's faithful steward, living in freedom from bondage and with an abundance of *true riches*.

Chuck Bentley
CEO of Crown Financial Ministries

Introduction

In *Freedom* I will be radically honest about my own adventure with faith and money. I will speak about my mistakes as well as my successes and how I'm learning to live my life for Jesus free from anxiety about money.

As a leader, I come across so many people who are anxious about money. A national poll by CreditCards.com surveyed 1,000 adults and two in three (sixty-five percent) of them said they lie awake at night fretting about money worries.

So if you have ever lost sleep over money you are certainly not alone. You are actually in the majority. Now that fact won't help you to stop losing sleep over money tonight or in the future but this book will.

As human beings we can only thrive when we live as we were designed to live. Whether we follow Jesus or not, the only way we can flourish and thrive is to follow God's instruction manual – namely the Bible.

Freedom will walk you through 10 Steps to ensure you can live your life for Jesus free from anxiety about money. Each Step includes a series of practical actions that you can immediately implement to ensure you are moving closer to living a life of financial freedom.

Matt Bird

matt@mattbirdspeaker.com
www.facebook.com/mattbirdspeaker
www.instagram.com/mattbirdspeaker
www.twitter.com/mattbirdspeaker
www.youtube.com/mattbirdspeaker
www.mattbirdspeaker.com

Step 1:
Decide to be financially free

"For where your treasure is, there your heart will be also... No one can serve two masters. Either you will hate the one and love the other, or you will be devoted to the one and despise the other. You cannot serve both God and money. Therefore I tell you, do not worry about your life, what you will eat or drink; or about your body, what you will wear. Is not life more than food, and the body more than clothes? Look at the birds of the air; they do not sow or reap or store away in barns, and yet your heavenly Father feeds them. Are you not much more valuable than they? Can any one of you by worrying add a single hour to your life?"

Matthew 6:21, 24-27

I grew up in a religious home. My father was a religious car washer. Every Sunday he would get a bucket of hot soapy water, a big sponge and wash his car and afterwards he would shammy it dry. My mum was a religious church goer. She would put on her Sunday best and walk to the church at the end of our street where she would sing hymns, listen to the preacher and say prayers. I always resented the fact that as a child I was made to follow my mum's religion rather than my dad's. I would have preferred to stay home and wash the family car rather than attend church and youth group every week.

Not having been a fan of school (or for that matter school certainly wasn't a fan of me) I left at the age of sixteen. Through a family friend I managed to secure a job in the Ministry of Defence which was a great start to working life. After five years, my career was developing very well working within a team on military technology to protect the country's national security.

Then I met a bunch of young people who loved Jesus. They made me feel rather uncomfortable in the way they talked about Jesus as if he were there in the moment with us. I decided to give Jesus a go and so one day I said a prayer and asked Jesus if he was real to make himself real to me. Well he certainly did. I was an extremely timid and uncertain person, however, knowing that Jesus not only loved me but also liked me was transformational. I became comfortable in my own skin and for the first time in my life became confident about who I was and discovered a powerful sense of God's purpose for my life.

I believed that God wanted me to go to Bible college and go on to be an evangelist and church planter so I handed in my resignation at work. When I told my parents, my mum was delighted but my father was furious, he said some things that I'm sure he didn't mean including that if I left my job I wasn't to come home again. It was hard for him to understand why anyone would give up a well-paid job with great career prospects out of a desire to tell the world about Jesus.

As I stepped into this next season of life I had to trust God to provide for me like I have never done before. I completed my studies at Bible college and became a church planter and evangelist with no regular income. Some people call it 'living by faith'. There were times of incredible provision when people gave me a car or sent a cheque that was for just the right amount.

I still 'live by faith' but nowadays it's to win commercial keynote speaking contracts, fund raise millions every year to employ people who work for my international non-profit organisation and also to support my ministry preaching, writing and broadcasting internationally. My commitments have dramatically increased, I have a wife and three children, a big mortgage and lots of people who rely on me for their income. I now need more faith than ever.

I have a high capacity for risk and lots of my friends tell me they couldn't live by faith in the way I do trusting for funding one month to the next in order to provide for my family and teams. I would be the first to say that there are times when I begin to lose my inner peace with God and start to panic. I start behaving as though I'm the provider rather than God. In those moments I, or more often my wife, remind me to get back to a place of surrender and peace.

Financial Freedom

Jesus invites us to live the great adventure of life with him free from concern about money, "Therefore I tell you, do not worry about your life, what you will eat or drink; or about your body, what you will wear." (Matthew 6:25). Woh, isn't that incredible? To be completely free from worry and anxiety about money, you have complete liberty to pursue whatever Jesus is asking of you. This kind of financial freedom must be possible otherwise Jesus would never have invited and encouraged us to live this way.

The life of financial freedom that Jesus calls us to is like the physical health that he wants for us, it doesn't just happen. If you want to be healthy it means developing the habits of eating well, exercising well, resting well, building healthy relationships and taking the advice of health professionals. In the same way that if you want financial health it means living a life surrendered to Jesus combined with disciplined habits about budgeting and income generation as well as giving generously, saving, and spending, and taking the advice of financial advisors. Financial freedom is not achieved by waving a magic wand but by taking a series of deliberate and disciplined steps, which is what this book is all about.

It is my experience that meaning in life is found not in what we get but in what we give. Some of the wealthiest people I have met are the least happy, with the least sense of life purpose. Some of the poorest people I have met are those who have the greatest sense of happiness and purpose. Jesus said, "Whoever wants to be my disciple must deny themselves and take up their cross daily and follow me. For whoever wants to save their life will lose it, but whoever loses their life for me will save it. What good is it for someone to gain the whole world, and yet lose or forfeit their very self?" (Luke 9:23-25). What Jesus says is such a powerful picture of what it looks like and feels like to live by faith free from concern about money.

How Much is Enough?

So how much money is enough for you to live free from anxiety? Major research has been undertaken into what level of income is needed for a person to be free from concern about money. In 2010, Daniel Kahneman (winner of the 2002 Nobel Prize for economics) and Angus Deaton (who later won the 2015 Noble Prize for economics) co-authored a study titled, 'High income improves evaluation of life but not emotional well-being'.

The study was based on 450,000 survey responses from Gallup and Healthways that sought to understand if there was a correlation between happiness and income. Deaton and Kahneman defined happiness in two ways, one being day-to-day 'emotional well-being' (how are you feeling today?) and the other 'life evaluation' (looking back on your life, how satisfied are you?).

The study found that the higher a persons income the more 'emotional well-being' they tended to report. This was only true up to a certain point, when annual income reached about $75,000. This makes sense because people earning significantly less than $75,000 are likely to spend a lot of their time being concerned about the basic needs of life, like paying the rent and having sufficient food to eat.

The survey also showed that more money does appear to increase 'life evaluation' without limit. Deaton and Kahneman concluded, 'high income buys life satisfaction but not happiness, and that low income is associated both with low life evaluation and low emotional well-being.'

In 2018, Purdue University and the University of Virginia used a survey of 1.7 million individuals from 164 countries to draw a correlation between happiness and income. The research calculated that $95,000 is an optimum salary for achieving life fulfilment for individuals. For simply achieving day-to-day feelings of happiness and well-being, as opposed to life satisfaction then $60,000 to $75,000 was estimated to be sufficient.

Andrew Jebb, lead author of the research paper 'Happiness, income satiation and turning points around the world,' said that, "Increases in happiness tend to diminish as you make more money." Jebb added, "A $20,000 increase from $30,000 to $50,000 is likely to bring more change to your life than if you make $20,000 on top of $150,000." This more recent research very much aligns with that carried out by Deaton and Kahneman.

So it could be argued that financial freedom, or the ability to live life without anxiety about money is achieved with an income of $75,000. Although this is a priviledged perspective given global poverty levels.

Enough is a very relative amount. In the 1980s, a group of economists at the World Bank observed that a number of countries drew their poverty line at a level of $370 dollars per annum. Later one of that group of economists called Martin Ravallion thought to divide $370 by 365 days and the concept of '$1 a day' was born, which became a powerful message for anti-poverty campaigners. One of the United Nations Millennium Development Goals aimed to halve the number of people living on $1 a day by 2015. The goal was nearly achieved, in 1990, 31% of the population of the developing world lived on less than $1 a day – close to 1.4 billion and in 2008, half that proportion did – 14%, or about 800 million.

The $1 a day figure is now seen as a bit arbitrary and the World Bank has developed stronger data around a level of $1.25 in a developing country and $2.5 in a developed country. In 2008, World Bank Development Indicators showed that, 'Almost half the world – over three billion people – live on less than $2.50 a day. At least 80% of humanity lives on less than $10 a day.' Whether the amount is $1, $1.25 or $2.5 this is still desperate poverty.

The Seduction

The challenge is that money and things are extremely seductive. The more we have the more we want. No matter how much money people have they normally believe that they would be happier and would have achieved a level of financial security if they just had a little bit more.

There is an urban myth about some market research which asked people how much they thought 'enough' money would be and at every income level they said about 20% more would be enough. As Biblical wisdom explains, "Whoever loves money never has enough; whoever loves wealth is never satisfied with their income. This too is meaningless." (Ecclesiastes 5:10). Money can be extremely seductive and it's too easy to believe that financial security would be achieved with more than you currently have.

Money wants to be our God, it wants us to love it and what it can do for us. This is why Jesus doesn't ask us to put God first and money second. Jesus is clear that we have a binary choice between either serving God or serving money. You can choose God or money but not both. Serving God is an act of worship and as Paul describes, "to offer your bodies as a living sacrifice, holy and pleasing to God – this is your true and proper worship." (Romans 12:1). The problem with being a living sacrifice is that it is all too easy to wriggle off the alter.

As a young leader I had the opportunity of spending a day with the international speaker, Luis Palau. There were twenty young leaders in the room and I was privileged to be one of them. I remember as if it were yesterday him taking a wad of money out of his pocket and waving it in the air explaining that money is not a problem, it's our relationship with it that matters. The desire for money can cause us to veer away from our faith, as Paul writes to Timothy, "For the love of money is a root of all kinds of evil. Some people, eager for money, have wandered from the faith and pierced themselves with many griefs." (1 Timothy 6:10).

Financial freedom is not about how much money we have. If we are in a place of financial hardship it's hard not to worry about money and be distracted by it because of our genuine need. Or if we are in a place of financial abundance then it's hard not to worry that we are doing the right thing with the resources we have and potentially be distracted in that way. Financial freedom is about having an undivided heart for Jesus and the ability to pursue him and his purposes without concern about money.

The Bible encourages us to be content, "But godliness with contentment is great gain," (1 Timothy 6:6) and, "Keep your lives free from the love of money and be content with what you have" (Hebrews 13:5). It's not about how much money we have but the degree to which we can live a life surrendered to Jesus regardless of how much money is in play.

Creation vs Materialism

God created the world in which we live; the sounds, the colours, the flavours, they are to be enjoyed. The Bible says that, "God saw all that he had made and it was good." (Genesis 1:31). God created people in his image so we are also mini-creators. We create music, art, architecture, cuisine, transportation – some of it is beautiful and some of it is ugly, although that is a matter of opinion. All these things are good and made for the benefit and pleasure of humankind.

God does, however, warn that things can become too important. When he gave the Ten Commandments to Moses he said, "You shall have no other gods before a me. You shall not make for yourself an image in the form of anything in heaven above or on the earth beneath or in the waters below. You shall not bow down to them or worship them; for I, the Lord your God, am a jealous God." (Exodus 20:3-5). Anything that becomes more important to us than God is an idol whether material things, money or indeed people. What God desires from us most is a relationship in which he is our first love. Anything that takes our attention from him is an idol.

Just like money material things can become seductive, in that the more we have the more we want. There are a number of other distortions about faith and money that can unhelpfully and negatively influence us.

Blind Faith

Blind faith is when people believe God will provide for all their needs without having to do anything other than pray. If this is really how money works then there would never be a case of a child going hungry, becoming malnourished and dying of preventable diseases despite their prayers. Instead, millions of children continue to die of preventable diseases despite their prayers and the prayers of the global church.

It is not enough to simply have faith because the Bible tells us that faith without action is dead (James 2:17). To be financially free requires faith to surrender your life to Jesus and also to take the necessary action to ensure that your finances are in good order and those of your community, city and country so that there is never a case that someone has so little that they starve to death.

Poverty Mentality

Poverty mentality is when people believe that poverty is next to holiness and that wealth (measured as, any amount of money you have more than I have) is bad! It looks down on the rich on the assumption that they must have gotten their wealth exploitatively at someone else's expense or through ill-gotten means.

In some churches there is a 'treat them mean keep them keen' culture where leaders are expected to live less well than their congregations and people who work for charities in a similar vein are expected to 'walk with a limp'. People are looked down upon disapprovingly if they go on luxury holidays, drive a prestige car or eat in fine food restaurants. To be financially free is not about taking a vow of poverty but about taking a vow of trust in Jesus.

Prosperity Gospel

Prosperity gospel is when people believe that if they have the right sort of faith and give, they will be healthy and wealthy. Prosperity gospel preachers and teachers declare that God wants you to be wealthy and healthy only if you have faith (and also demonstrate that faith through making an appropriate offering to their ministry!) Tragically the target audience of such preaching and teaching is often on those people who can ill-afford to be exploited out of the little money they have.

Prosperity gospel teaching damages lives. At its best it leads to disappointment and self-blame. At its worst it causes people to give up on their faith because it doesn't work according to the formula they were taught and had modelled in front of their eyes. The prosperity gospel is a highly attractive promise particularly to vulnerable people who have very little but it is a distortion of the life of self-giving that Jesus lived and calls on us to.

Financial Religiosity

Financial religiosity is when people believe that there are strict boundaries on what people should and shouldn't do with their money. As with all religion it misses the heart of the matter and gets caught up with secondary issues. It has dogmatic beliefs that are quick to condemn people who do things it believes are wrong which may include gambling, smoking or shopping on a Sunday. Not that I am necessarily endorsing these things either!

Religious people define the wealthy as anyone who owns a bigger house, drives a bigger car or lives a bigger lifestyle than they do. They fail to recognise the relative nature of wealth and poverty because there is always someone who has more than you and always someone who has less than you. Financial religiosity, as with all forms of religion, is exactly what Jesus came to expose and supersede.

Financial freedom is quite different to blind faith, a poverty mentality, the prosperity gospel and financial religiosity.

Servant vs Master

Money is a liberating servant but it can also be a controlling master. Money can liberate us to pursue God and his purpose for our lives or alternatively it can seduce and enslave us and become our number one priority, in effect our 'god'. The Bible is not an advocate of blind faith, a poverty mentality, the prosperity gospel or financial religiosity, but an advocate for freedom. To be financially free means living life to the full following Jesus and his purpose for our life free from concern about money.

FREEDOM STEP 1

The first step to financial freedom is to ensure that your life is fully surrendered to Jesus and that you are committed to taking action to put your finances in order so that you can focus on pursuing God's calling on your life free from concern about money.

A) Write down what you believe Jesus is asking you to be and do for him (use a journal if you would like more space).

....

....

....

....

....

....

....

....

B) In what ways are your finances either enabling or inhibiting you to pursue that? What do your bank statements and credit card statements say about your faith?

....

....

....

....

C) Name the things that you need to change in order to be able to live life for Jesus free from concern about money.

....

....

....

....

Start taking action on these things now so that you can more easily live your life for Jesus.

D) Pray and dedicate yourself to pursuing Jesus and his desires for your life, whatever the cost. You may wish to use the Methodist Church 'Covenant' prayer:

> I am no longer my own but yours.
> Put me to what you will,
> rank me with whom you will;
> put me to doing,
> put me to suffering;
> let me be employed for you,
> or laid aside for you,
> exalted for you,
> or brought low for you;
> let me be full,
> let me be empty,
> let me have all things,
> let me have nothing:
> I freely and wholeheartedly yield all things
> to your pleasure and disposal.
> And now, glorious and blessed God,
> Father, Son and Holy Spirit,
> you are mine and I am yours. So be it.
> And the covenant now made on earth,
> let it be ratified in heaven.

Step 2:
Believe that God plans to prosper you

"This is what the Lord Almighty, the God of Israel, says to all those I carried into exile from Jerusalem to Babylon: 'Build houses and settle down; plant gardens and eat what they produce. Marry and have sons and daughters; find wives for your sons and give your daughters in marriage, so that they too may have sons and daughters. Increase in number there; do not decrease. Also, seek the peace and prosperity of the city to which I have carried you into exile. Pray to the Lord for it, because if it prospers, you too will prosper.' Yes, this is what the Lord Almighty, the God of Israel, says: 'Do not let the prophets and diviners among you deceive you. Do not listen to the dreams you encourage them to have. They are prophesying lies to you in my name. I have not sent them,' declares the Lord. This is what the Lord says: 'When seventy years are completed for Babylon, I will come to you and fulfil my good promise to bring you back to this place. For I know the plans I have for you,' declares the Lord, 'plans to prosper you and not to harm you, plans to give you hope and a future. Then you will call on me and come and pray to me, and I will listen to you. You will seek me and find me when you seek me with all your heart. I will be found by you,' declares the Lord, 'and will bring you back from captivity. I will gather you from all the nations and places where I have banished you,' declares the Lord, 'and will bring you back to the place from which I carried you into exile.'"

Jeremiah 29:4-14

I had been involved in the leadership of a UK mission mobilisation initiative which on completion had admirably commissioned an independent review of its impact. One of the points of feedback was that the initiative had failed to engage effectively with black majority churches. Given that there are more black Christians in London than white Christians this was not insignificant feedback.

We decided to start by addressing the make-up of the national leadership team which was a 'whitewash'. It was agreed that I should invite two black leaders to a meeting with a view to them joining the team. The meeting went very well, it involved some honest conversations about how an exclusively white-led initiative can invite black churches to be involved and then be surprised when they do not respond positively.

Once the two guests had departed the conversation continued about whether they should be invited to join the team. Disappointingly, the conversation that followed made some assumptions. There was concern that if the two gentleman were involved then the churches that we were already working with might become 'contaminated with the prosperity gospel'. This discussion revealed a deep prejudice about black churches and an assumption that because black faith talks about money more than white churches then they believe in the prosperity gospel.

When your community are over-represented amongst those who are unemployed and in low paid jobs, in prisons and mental health institutions, and in fact on virtually every other negative social metrics you could name, you cannot afford for the gospel to be about spiritual salvation alone. In these circumstances you are hungry for something or someone who can transform your current reality.

Platitudes about riches in heaven when you die while you are struggling to put food on the table for your family in the here and now is not 'good news to the poor' (Luke 4:18). Only middle income and middle class Christianity can afford for the gospel to be about spiritual salvation alone. People living in poverty need good news that can transform their situation in the here and now and not just in heaven when they die.

What can be perceived as churches advocating the prosperity gospel can actually be churches providing hope and a message of economic empowerment. When you have no food to feed your family or you are in a low-paid job your need is economic hope. Jesus teaches that eternal life starts today not on the day we die. There is a critical difference between the 'prosperity gospel' which promises health and wealth and 'economic empowerment' that offers financial freedom and liberation in the midst of hardship and poverty.

If you are reading this and think that I am saying that Jesus makes you rich please go back and reread what you've read. What to the privileged may sound like the prosperity gospel to the poor is a gospel of hope. Jesus wants to economically empower people to have the confidence to apply for a job, or give them the vision to start a small business or to challenge prejudice and racism in the workplace that keeps them out of senior positions and the boardroom. God wants all people to be able to flourish and provide for their families.

There is also a challenge here about how we talk about money in church. All leaders should talk about money but in such a way as to avoid any misunderstanding that you should 'pray and God will make you rich'.

God wants to Prosper You

If you are out of work, God would love you to get a job. If you are in a low paid job, God would love to see you earn the minimum wage. If your small business is struggling, God would love to see it turn around. If you are failing to achieve your targets, God would love to see you achieve a breakthrough. If you are the victim of prejudice, God desires that you experience justice.

God wants to prosper you, this is NOT the same as getting rich, it is about being able to provide for yourself and your family and achieve a level of well-being. There is no dignity in long-term hand outs from government, charity or family when you have the potential to work for a living. God wants to economically empower you.

Prophet Jeremiah

Warcraft teaches that one of the ways to suppress a nation when you have beaten them in battle is to remove its leaders. The nation of Israel had been unfaithful in her relationship with God and aroused his anger and so he had allowed the Babylonians to beat her in battle and take control of their capital city Jerusalem. In order to maintain control, the Babylonians began a process of exiling Jerusalem's leaders to Babylon.

Israel was in a dark and difficult place, she had been beaten in battle and her victor was now completely destabilising her society by exiling her leaders. Israel was left wondering where God was in all that was happening and whether he still had a plan for them as his chosen people. God, in his incredible compassion and grace, spoke through his prophet Jeremiah with a message of hope and a promise that he would prosper them, "'For I know the plans I have for you,' declares the Lord, 'plans to prosper you and not to harm you, plans to give you hope and a future.'" (Jeremiah 29:11). Jeremiah is a powerful example of God's intention to prosper us holistically in four dimensions; spiritual, social, economic and political.

Spiritual Intent

God had previously sent Jeremiah to warn Israel, "Turn now, each of you, from your evil ways… and you can stay in the land the Lord gave to you… Do not follow other gods to worship and serve them… Then I will not harm you." (Jeremiah 25:5-6). Then God's patience ran out and he said, "But you did not listen… you have aroused my anger… I will summon the people of the north… I will bring them against this land… I will completely destroy them' (Jeremiah 25:7-9)."

Now all that God had warned would happen as a result of Israels unfaithfulness had come to pass. Israel was destroyed and her leaders were being exiled to Babylon. Despite all that had happened God had not given up on Israel, more than anything else he wanted a relationship with her. So yet again God spoke and reached out to Israel through Jeremiah saying, "This is what the Lord Almighty, the God of Israel, says."

(Jeremiah 29:4). Whatever happens, whether we are obedient or disobedient, God never stops speaking and desiring a relationship with us.

From the creation of the world, God has desired one thing, that his people would be in a faithful relationship with him. Through the patriarchs and the prophets, priests and kings God spoke consistently to Israel to woo and invite her into a faithful relationship. God's people then and God's people now struggle to sustain that trusting faithful relationship with him.

We find it difficult to trust someone that we can't see. We struggle with uncertainty. Not knowing is one of the most difficult aspects of life. So we clamour and grasp for certainty wherever we can find it. We end up taking hold of things and idolising them because we can see them, touch them and feel them. So we snatch at what is created rather the creator himself. God calls us to live a life in step with his spirit to accept his love, receive his guidance and trust in his provision.

King Solomon put it so very well when he said, "Trust in the Lord with all your heart and lean not on your own understanding; in all your ways submit to him and he will make your paths straight." (Proverbs 3:5-6). One of the words that I have found very helpful in describing this invisible trusting relationship with God is relinquishment. For me relinquishment to God is a live project, I am constantly wrestling and resting to try and ensure my life is lived surrendered to God. It means I put the best of who I am into everything I do, and at the same time relinquishing to God the outcome of what he will actually accomplish and achieve through it. Keep working on your live project, believe that God wants to strengthen your relationship with him.

Financial Intent

God taught Israel that to prosper meant having a right relationship with money. Jeremiah said, "Build houses and settle down; plant gardens and eat what they produce." (Jeremiah 29:5). Even though God's people were refugees living in a foreign city God told them that they should invest their capital and they should grow their incomes. It would have been tempting for Israel to believe that there was no point in trying to flourish financially because their current predicament was hopeless and temporary.

Sometimes people of faith live as if this world is temporary and so it matters little about what happens other than you survive until you get to heaven. The Bible, however, tells us another story, it doesn't talk about going to heaven but about heaven coming to earth.

For example, "Your Kingdom come, your will be done, on earth as it is in heaven," (Matthew 6:10) and "I saw the Holy City, the new Jerusalem, coming down out of heaven from God." (Revelation 21:2). So life on earth may not be as temporary as we are sometimes led to believe. The Bible also tells us that God is regenerating creation, "We know that the whole creation has been groaning as in the pains of childbirth right up to the present time," (Romans 8:22), so God clearly has a purpose for it. It would be awfully bad stewardship to simply throw the world away and besides that, God has promised never to destroy the world again: "Never again will the waters become a flood to destroy all life." (Genesis 9:15). Life on earth may be longer than we think, it may be where heaven is established and where eternity is located.

When I was studying for my masters degree in missiology, the study of the mission of God, I remember examining a phenomena known as 'Redemption and Lift'. The phrase 'Redemption and Lift' was coined by missiologist Donald McGavran which explained that when people became followers of Jesus they experienced greater social mobility and economic improvement – in other words they become more middle class and financially better off. Some of my fellow students viewed this as a missiological problem whereas clearly this is the gospel at work.

The Distinguished Professor of the Social Sciences at Baylor University and founding editor of the *Interdisciplinary Journal of Research on Religion*, Rodney Stark, provides statistical evidence for 'Redemption and Lift'. He explains that people of faith:

- engage in less criminal behaviour and more pro-social behaviour
- experience higher marital happiness and lower divorce rates, while producing more and better-behaved children
- report more and better sex with their spouse, and less cheating
- experience better mental health, and probably better physical health too
- give more generously in terms of money and time
- and are better educated and more successful.

This happens because when you follow Jesus there are lots of ways he changes you. You become more comfortable in your own skin and who God has made you to be. You become more loving, caring a considerate about others. You become more honest and ask ethical questions about life and work. You become more motivated, passionate and purposeful. You become more of a social creature building relationships with people in the church and wider community. You begin the journey of becoming a better version of yourself.

In life you become better at building relationships. You are encouraged to enrich your marriage, you are supported through difficult seasons. You develop a stronger ability to build relationships with people who are unlike you. So you become upwardly socially mobile. At work you are asked to take on new responsibilities, you are given promotion, you apply for new jobs and your income increases.

So 'Redemption and Lift' is actually God causing his people to thrive.

Social Intent

God encouraged his people to build relational and social capital, "Marry and have sons and daughters; find wives for your sons and give your daughters in marriage, so that they too may have sons and daughters. Increase in number there; do not decrease." (Jeremiah 29:6).

Relationships are central to how God blesses and favours you. A Mental Health Foundation report 'Relationships in the 21st century' explains, "People who are more socially connected to family, friends, or their community are happier, physically healthier and live longer, with fewer mental health problems than people who are less well connected." It doesn't get more straightforward than that. Invest in healthy relationships and you will have a healthier life.

We really shouldn't be surprised. God is one, and he is three persons, the Father, Son and Holy Spirit. God's very identity is one of relationships and we are created in his image so we are also made for relationships. In fact we can only flourish and thrive as a human being in relationships with other people. A significant part of what it means to prosper is to enjoy healthy relationships.

Relationships also help us prosper at work. The job recruitment sector explains that building the right relationships will help you get on in your career. The 'hidden job market' explains that two thirds of jobs are never advertised because they go to people already known by the employer.

When you think about it, it makes complete sense. It's always safer to give a job to someone you've worked with before, who you know is good at what they do. Going to the open job market is full of risks. You can rigorously vet application letters and CVs, ask great questions at interviews, run assessment centres and still end up recruiting people who can't do the job.

Relationships are also the fastest, easiest and simplest way to get anything done. It doesn't matter how outstanding your organisational policies, procedures and systems are, if you know someone who can help you that will always be the best way to get anything done.

Our commitment to building social and relational capital determines how much God is able to prosper us.

Political Intent

God encouraged his people to engage in their municipality, "Seek the peace and prosperity of the city… Pray to the Lord for it, because if it prospers, you too will prosper." (Jeremiah 29:7).

When I studied theology I remember being told that the Romans and Pharisees were threatened by Jesus because they mistakenly thought he was a political leader who had come to undermine, disrupt and usurp their power. They went on to explain that Jesus' Kingdom was not an earthly Kingdom but a heavenly, eternal and spiritual Kingdom and so the Romans and Pharisees were mistaken. I now think that was a load of rubbish.

Politics at its most rudimentary is the way that we choose to live together as a society so that all can thrive. So of course Jesus was a political leader, he has everything to say about how we choose to live together as a society. How on earth could the creator of the universe not have a view about how his creation chooses to live together as a society.

As the founder of Cinnamon International I have been deeply involved in church-led community transformation projects that reduce antisocial behaviour, provide emergency food parcels, help resettle refugees, visit the vulnerable elderly, mentor young people at risk of exclusion from school and address many other social issues. While each project offers very practical help, you might call it social action, the secret to every project is the relationships that are built. Whenever you talk to a beneficiary, what they talk about the most isn't the help but the helper, not the favour but the friendship they found that gave them the resilience to transform their situation.

Most people will never be homeless because while they may lose their job or suffer a marriage breakup they will have a friend who would let them sleep on their sofa or in their spare room. The people who do end up homeless are those people who, for many complicated reasons, don't have that social infrastructure in their lives or those relationships have become highly dysfunctional.

Our faith has everything to say about how we choose to live together as a society. God wants all people to engage politically by pursuing the peace and prosperity of their municipality. Some people do that by serving as a politician, others by serving a politician and others through conversation, voting and action.

We will thrive most when we politically engage by pursuing the peace and prosperity of our municipality. God has hardwired creation so we will only flourish, thrive and prosper when we live in a society that pursues the wellbeing of all not the wellbeing of self.

Over Spiritualised, Futurised & Individualised

One of the greatest obstacles to prospering as God wants us to prosper is perversely faith, because it has become distorted in three ways. Firstly, our faith has become over spiritualised because faith has been reduced to a spiritual realm which has little connection with social, financial and political aspects of life. Faith has become a body of knowledge rather than a way of life. Gnosticism was an early church heresy based on the belief that secret knowledge would allow you to transcend into the spiritual realm. Some Bible teaching today sounds strangely like that ancient Gnostic heresy.

Secondly, our faith has become over futurised because faith has become focused and sometimes limited to what happens when we die rather than what we do today and everyday. Faith has been reduced to a transaction that gets us into heaven when we die rather than an experience of the holistic transformation of Jesus today.

Finally, our faith has become over individualised because faith has been reduced to the individual choices we make rather than the collective choices we make and identity we have together. There is no doubt that we each have responsibility for our own decisions, however, there is also a strong theme within the Bible about God's intention for the collective. After all, God puts the lonely in families, asks us to pursue the peace and prosperity of cities, and he transforms communities, baptises households, commands us to disciple nations and calls us as he has done to love the world.

So let's recognise, accept and embrace the holistic, immediate and collective power of our faith so that we can flourish in God.

FREEDOM STEP 2

The second step to financial freedom is to believe and trust that God plans for you to prosper, flourish and thrive in every aspect of your life; spiritually, socially, economically and politically.

People with a plan are more successful than those without a plan. People who write their plan down are more successful than those that don't. People who have smart goals are more successful than those who do not. People who develop daily habits towards their goals are more successful than those who do not.

A) Write down a spiritual, relational, financial and civic goal that you believe Jesus desires to achieve in and through you.

Spiritual ....

....

....

....

Relational ....

....

....

....

Financial ....

....

....

....

Civic ....

....

B) Write down the first three actions that you could take towards achieving each of these goals.

Spiritual

1] ....

2] ....

3] ....

Relational

1] ....

2] ....

3] ....

Financial

1] ....

2] ....

3] ....

Civic

1] ....

2] ....

3] ....

C) What new daily lifestyle habits would help you to take these actions and achieve these goals?

....

....

....

....

....

D) Ask someone you know well who is also pursuing Jesus if they would be your accountability partner. Explain your plan to them and ask if they would encourage, pray and challenge you on the journey. Who might that person be?

....

....

....

....

....

....

....

....

....

....

Step 3:
Recognise everything you have is God's

"Then the leaders of families, the officers of the tribes of Israel, the commanders of thousands and commanders of hundreds, and the officials in charge of the king's work gave willingly. They gave toward the work on the temple of God five thousand talents and ten thousand darics of gold, ten thousand talents of silver, eighteen thousand talents of bronze and a hundred thousand talents of iron. Anyone who had precious stones gave them to the treasury of the temple of the Lord in the custody of Jehiel the Gershonite. The people rejoiced at the willing response of their leaders, for they had given freely and wholeheartedly to the Lord. David the king also rejoiced greatly... But who am I, and who are my people, that we should be able to give as generously as this? Everything comes from you, and we have given you only what comes from your hand."

1 Chronicles 29:6-9 & 14

Since my children were young I have raised them playing 'fire-side games'. These are the small games that live under the coffee table in our sitting room. Games like tiddly winks, pick up sticks, snap, dice words and pass the pigs. On wet and cold days, of which the UK has plenty, we light the log fire and play 'fire-side games'.

While the children are a bit older now we still play daddy's 'fireside games' but more often we are playing more complicated board games. On those wet and cold days one of the children's favourite games is Monopoly. The big downside is that it can take forever to play so I have tweaked the game a little to speed up play.

We pick our characters and then we are off. We race round the board trying to earn as much money as possible and pay as few fines and taxes as possible. Then we start buying houses and other assets in order to try and get ahead of the other people in the game. In some ways Monopoly is sadly just like life.

A wise friend once said, "Life is like a game of Monopoly, at the end of the game all the pieces go back in the box." As the book of Job explains so well, "Naked I came from my mother's womb, and naked I will depart." (Job 1:21) and as the apostle Paul taught his mentee, Timothy, "For we brought nothing into the world, and we can take nothing out of it." (1 Timothy 6:7). I met a gentleman recently who keeps a jar of earth on his bedside table to remind him that he came into the world with nothing and will leave the world with nothing.

So if we start life with nothing and we end life with nothing then surely that changes what we do with what happens in the middle. Whether you have a faith that believes in life after death or not, the fact that you start with nothing and end with nothing begs the question, how are you going to treat what you have in the middle?

Ownership

God owns 100% of who we are and what we have. So anything we give to him, or give in service to him is his already and anything we keep hold of we are merely managing on his behalf. This is exactly what David declared on behalf of Israel to God, "Everything comes from you, and we have given you only what comes from your hand." (1 Chronicles 29:14).

In the words of the former Dutch Prime Minister Abraham Kuyper, "There is not a square inch in the whole domain of our human existence over which Christ, who is Sovereign over all, does not cry: 'Mine!'" God's total ownership over everything that exists is a clear theme within the Bible...

"The earth is the Lord's, and everything in it, the world, and all who live in it." (Psalm 24:1)

"The land must not be sold permanently, because the land is mine and you reside in my land as foreigners and strangers." (Leviticus 25:23)

"Everything under heaven belongs to me." (Job 41:11b)

"The silver is mine and the gold is mine,' declares the Lord Almighty." (Haggai 2:8)

"Do you not know that your bodies are temples of the Holy Spirit, who is in you, whom you have received from God? You are not your own; you were bought at a price. Therefore honour God with your bodies." (1 Corinthians 6:19-20)

If God owns everything that exists it means that we are owned by him and everything that we think is ours we are only managing and stewarding on his behalf.

Stewardship

In the beginning God gave people stewardship responsibility for looking after creation. "God blessed them and said to them, 'Be fruitful and increase in number; fill the earth and subdue it. Rule over the fish of the sea and the birds in the sky and over every living creature that moves the ground.'" (Genesis 1:28). The word 'rule', or 'dominion' as used in other translations, means to manage, which is not about ownership but about looking after something on behalf of someone else.

God spoke to Abraham and invited him on an adventure to enter a promised land, "Go from your country, your people and your father's household to the land I will show you." (Genesis 12:1-14). God promised his people the land as their possession, "The whole land of Canaan, where you now reside as a foreigner, I will give you as an everlasting possession to you and your descendants after you." (Genesis 17:8). It was a possession that God's people would manage rather than own as Leviticus makes clear, "The land must not be sold permanently, because the land is mine and you reside in my land as foreigners and strangers." (Leviticus 25:23). While God's people were offered this promised land as their possession and inheritance it was theirs to look after and God's to own.

Through Moses, God promised his people that the land would be "flowing with milk and honey," (Exodus 3:8) because with land comes great prosperity. Land can be fertile with many crops, it contains animals for sustenance and contains natural resources which can be harvested. This is why throughout human history people, tribes and nations have fought one another for territory. Through Moses, God was promising his people that they would prosper greatly.

In the time of King David, Israel was living in the promised land and was building a temple in honour of God. As we read at the beginning of this chapter, David gathered the tribes of Israel and made a compelling case for funding the temple. His appeal ended with the unforgettable words, "Everything comes from you, and we have given you only what comes from your hand." (1 Chronicles 29:14). Here again there is an understanding of stewardship that everything we have is God's and we are only looking after it.

The New Testament continues this theme of responsibility and stewardship for what God has given into our care. Jesus said, "But to the one who does not know and does things deserving punishment will be beaten with few blows. From everyone who has been given much, much will be demanded; and from the one who has been entrusted with much, much more will be asked." (Luke 12:48). There is a strong accountability to God for what we have and a correlation between God's blessing and God's expectations.

The apostle Paul advocates the principle of sowing and reaping or to put it another way what you give in life determines what you get out of life. He says, "Remember this: Whoever sows sparingly will also reap sparingly; and whoever sows generously will also reap generously. Each of you should give what you have decided in your heart to give, not reluctantly or under compulsion, for God loves a cheerful giver."(2 Corinthians 9:6-7).

The apostle Peter emphasises that stewardship is not only of money but of gifts and abilities, "Each of you should use whatever gift you have received to serve others, as faithful stewards of God's grace in its various forms." (1 Peter 4:10).

A Biblical understanding of ownership and stewardship transforms our attitude to what we have because whether we have a little or a lot is not important, it's what we do with what we have that matters.

God's Resources

God is the source of all our resources, everything that we have originates from him. We are stewards of the money that he has entrusted to us, we are stewards of the gifts and abilities that we have been given. We are stewards of each moment that we live and breathe and we are also stewards of the relationships that God has given us.

Time

Time is one of the most precious assets we have. You can never regain time you have spent and it's one of the few things that money can't buy.

The greatest consumer of our time is probably our work. It is likely that we spend more waking hours at work than we do anything else in our lives. So if we want to be good stewards of our time what we do for work really matters. Our time at work is an opportunity to contribute to the mission of God in the world. I meet so many people who feel trapped at work rather than liberated at work. If you do not believe that God is in your work don't waste another hour of your time – please find God in your work or find new work.

There are number of distractions that can eat huge chunks of our time. Church meetings are a big one. I've been in churches where you are encouraged to be part of so many activities that if you got sucked in you'd have no time left to be with your family and friends and influence the world around you. Another huge time consumer is digital entertainment, it is so easy to watch television every night and spend hours every day on social media when instead you could be spending time with people.

Life is fragile, you never know when your final day will come so steward your time well. Think about how you can spend your time to do the things that really matter to you and God. At the end of life I have never heard that anyone has said that they wish they had spent more time at the office, in church meetings or watching television.

Talents

It is easy to say 'we are all good at something' and I truly believe we are, however, it can sometimes take years to discover what you are uniquely good at.

The Gallup Organisation is best known for its surveys but it is also a world leader on research about people and talent. The book *Now, Discover Your Strengths* describes talent as the things we cannot help but do, they are easy and we do them consistently without thinking.

Another Gallup book *StrengthsFinder* describes thirty-four strengths but more powerfully provides a unique code that enables you to complete an online questionnaire to help you identify your strengths. The survey will play back to you what it believes are your top five strength areas, when I completed this questionnaire the results certainly resonated with me.

Of course completing a questionnaire isn't the only way you can discover your talents. Life experience is one of the most powerful ways to discover what you are good at. I remember the day when I had been to meet an influential political leader and gained their support for an initiative. Afterwards it dawned on me that I had a special knack for building relationships and influencing them to support particular causes. I felt enormously liberated knowing that whatever I did in life I should use this talent which would cause me to flourish and thrive.

Another way of discovering our talents is to ask our friends. Sometimes we are so close to our own talents that we can't see them and the effect they have on other people. Explaining to a small number of people who know us well that we are exploring our talents and asking them what they think we are good at will be sure to produce some insights that are well worth exploring.

Treasure

Part of our responsibility as followers of Jesus is to generously give treasure/money to him and his work. We shall explore different models for generous giving in Chapter 8: Reflect God through your generosity, but let's take the most commonly practiced model of giving, a tithe or 10% of our earnings, for the sake of this conversation.

God is interested in what we do with everything we have. Generously giving 10% of our earnings to God does not immunise him from an interest in what we do with the other 90%. God is not looking for religious observance he is looking for a relationship of love and devotion. The Old Testament prophets were hot on this. They made really clear that God is not interested in empty religious acts and offerings:

"For I desire mercy, not sacrifice, and acknowledgment of God rather than burnt offerings." (Hosea 6:6)

"Though you bring choice fellowship offerings, I will have no regard for them. Away with the noise of your songs! I will not listen to the music of your harps. But let justice roll on like a river, righteousness like a never-failing stream!" (Amos 5:22b-24)

God is not interested in us going through the motions he wants a heart connection with us that has a transformative impact on our lives and on the world around us. God is not looking for a 'tip' of 10% like we would give to a waiter in a restaurant. God wants us to recognise that everything we earn belongs to him, that all our financial resources are on loan to us from him and we are managers and guardians.

So the money that we put in the offering on Sunday (or the standing order equivalent) is only the beginning of the story. God is interested in what we do with our financial resources Monday to Saturday. Do we squander what God has given us or are we wise and leverage them for maximum effect.

Trust

Recently I talked over lunch with Mart Green who is part of the Hobby Lobby family business in the United States. Each week I publish a 60 second video 'A Minute with Matt' about someone I've met and something I've learnt from them about relationships, so I was keen to pick up an insight from Mart. As we talked about generosity he commented that alongside our time, talent and treasure one of the most valuable resources we can be generous with is the trust we have built with other people. Introducing people to people can be a powerful act of generosity helping people make friends, meet Mr or Mrs right, get jobs, win contracts and many other life opportunities. There was my 'A Minute with Matt' right there.

Relationology International is the company I started that is dedicated to growing leaders, teams and business through the power of relationships. I believe the true currency of business is relationships and not money because when given the choice, people choose to work with people they know, like and trust rather than the people they don't. Trust increases performance because trusting relationships are the fastest, simplest and easiest way to get anything done. It doesn't matter what procedures and systems an organisation has in place, trust is what enables you to get things done. So who we trust and who trusts us is one of the most powerful life and marketplace assets we have.

God is a God of relationships and having been created in his image we are also made for relationships. The Bible, from Genesis to Revelation, is a book about humanity's relationship with and trust in God, and also relationship with one another. So the Bible is a book about relationships not a book about religion.

The Bible explains that we are stewards of everything in our lives including our relationships and the trust we build within those relationships. So these relationships are not our possessions, we do not own them, we are stewards of them. If that is the case we should be generous with the trust we are building and share our relationships with other people.

God invites us to be stewards of all the time, talents, treasure and trust that he has given into our care.

Rewards

As a younger leader I was privileged to share a speaking platform with a highly respected leader and theologian. We were speaking about faith and money. He leant over to me and said, "Matt, remember we are saved by grace but rewarded by works."

The apostle Paul made very clear that we are accepted by God because of his generosity not our goodness, "For it is by grace that you have been saved through faith – and this is not from yourselves, it is the gift of God – not by works so that no one can boast. For we are God's handiwork, created in Christ Jesus to do good works, which God prepared in advance for us to do." (Ephesians 2:8-9). As the Great Reformation declares *Sola Fide,* by faith alone.

Paul also explained that we would receive an inheritance and reward in proportion to our works, "Whatever you do, work at it with all your heart, as working for the Lord, not for men, since you know that you will receive an inheritance from the Lord as a reward." (Colossians 3:23-24). So once we have decided to follow Jesus how we steward what he gives us determines the reward we will receive from him.

So good stewardship will lead to a good reward, great stewardship will lead to a great reward and awesome stewardship to an awesome reward.

FREEDOM STEP 3

The third step to financial freedom is to recognise that everything you have is God's and that although you may be managing it, you are not its owner. Undertake a stewardship audit to more fully understand and appreciate what God has already entrusted you to look after.

A) Time: What are the three greatest chunks of time that you have in your life to utilise for God?

1] ....

2] ....

3] ....

B) Talent: What are the three things that you find easier, can do faster and that you get more enjoyment from than other people?

1] ....

2] ....

3] ....

C) Treasure: What are the three most significant financial resources and assets that God has entrusted to your care?

1] ....

2] ....

3] ....

D) Trust: Who are the three individuals or groups of people that God has given you favour and trust with?

1] ....

2] ....

3] ....

E) Pray surrendering these resources to God knowing that you are merely the steward of them and not the owner of them.

F) Configure (or reconfigure) your life to ensure that you are using these resources and assets on a regular basis to pursue Jesus and what he has asked you to be and do with your life. What adjustments might you want to make?

....

....

....

Step 4:
Ask God for the gift of wealth creation

"When you have eaten and are satisfied, praise the Lord your God for the good land he has given you. Be careful that you do not forget the Lord your God, failing to observe his commands, his laws and his decrees that I am giving you this day. Otherwise, when you eat and are satisfied, when you build fine houses and settle down, and when your herds and flocks grow large and your silver and gold increase and all you have is multiplied, then your heart will become proud and you will forget the Lord your God, who brought you out of Egypt, out of the land of slavery. He led you through the vast and dreadful wilderness, that thirsty and waterless land, with its venomous snakes and scorpions. He brought you water out of hard rock. He gave you manna to eat in the wilderness, something your ancestors had never known, to humble and test you so that in the end it might go well with you. You may say to yourself, 'My power and the strength of my hands have produced this wealth for me.' But remember the Lord your God, for it is he who gives you the ability to produce wealth, and so confirms his covenant, which he swore to your ancestors, as it is today."

Deuteronomy 8:10-18

My first business enterprise emerged when I was still at school. Most of my friends at school used to get up at 5am in the morning six days a week to deliver newspapers and get paid not very much. I'm sure it could have been fun in the summer but those mornings with rain, ice or snow must have been miserable. Such a job had no appeal to me and besides that I thought I could earn better money.

My father worked for a food and beverages business and once a week he would go to the staff shop and get some goodies at a knock down price. So every day I would go to school with a packed lunch that included a chocolate bar. One day a boy in my class called Barney, who saw me eating my chocolate asked if he could buy it from me. Well why not.

My school had a rule that you couldn't leave the premises to go to the local shop at lunch time and if you did you got an after school detention. So I wondered if more children would be interested in buying a chocolate bar from me and avoid the risk of a detention. So the next day I went to school with a handful of chocolate bars and I sold them immediately.

The day after I took a whole box of chocolate bars in my sports bag and quickly sold everyone of them at morning break time. Now I had a supply challenge so I had to persuade my dad to go into his staff shop every day and buy me boxes of chocolate bars. I think the people who worked in the shop must have thought my dad had an awful lot of children.

I had stumbled across a great little business. The children in my class were able to buy great chocolate at a better price than the local shop and at the same time avoid the risk of getting a detention. My chocolate enterprise only took ten minutes of my mid-morning break at school. I made 60% profit on what I sold and was earning in a day what it took the other children a week to earn. It also saved me doing one of those wretched paper rounds.

That experience and other such ventures gave me an early taste for entrepreneurial ways of generating income. I have been running my own businesses ever since. It's not necessarily about becoming rich but it's hugely satisfying to be able to generate your own livelihood from scratch and if God does bless your ventures you will have immense pleasure in deploying those resources for the Kingdom of God.

God-Made

I love reading autobiographies and biographies, learning peoples life stories and discovering how they become successful. Many of them claim to be 'self-made' but they really aren't. Without exception, they all share the same secret to success. Most of the biographies are not explicit about it but all of them say the same thing implicitly. The secret to their success was their relationships. There are people who they met along the way who helped them and without their assistance they would never have succeeded. People are never so good that they can succeed without the help of others and none of us should forget that.

In the same way we should remember that none of us succeeds financially without the help of others. The Bible says, "But remember the Lord your God, for it is he who gives you the ability to produce wealth." (Deuteronomy 8:18). So there is no such thing as a 'self-made' man or woman only a 'God-made' man or woman.

Wealth creation is like all other God-given gifts. You may find your already have the gift and it's about developing it to its maximum potential. Alternatively if you don't have the gift and you would like to ask God if he would give it to you, Jesus said, "Ask and it will be given to you." (Matthew 7:7). Paul urged the Church in the city of Corinth, "eagerly desire gifts of the Spirit," (1 Corinthians 14:1) and James said, "If any of you lacks wisdom, you should ask God, who gives generously to all without finding fault, and it will be given to you." (James 1:5). So if you would like to be able to create wealth and understand the responsibilities that come with it ask God for the gift.

Next begin to exercise the gift, it's a bit like going to the gym in order to get fit, tone your body or build muscle. The experts say that it takes 10,000 hours of practice to move from being a novice to becoming a master at something. So take every opportunity to increase your flying hours. Recently I was on a long haul flight which, when it landed, it was announced we had been flown by the airlines most senior pilot and that he had flown for tens of thousands of hours and the equivalent of numerous times around the world. Experience counts for a lot.

If you would like God to make you a wealth creator pray all you like but you are also going to need to work like your life depended on it. I have never met someone who has created wealth who did not have to work day and night for years to build a successful enterprise. As Biblical wisdom says, "All hard work brings a profit, but mere talk leads only to poverty." (Proverbs 14:23). So at some point the talk has to stop and the real work has to begin.

You might like to identify a number of people who are on the same journey of developing the gift of wealth creation and ask them to form a group together. You could also identify someone who is a successful wealth creator and build a relationship with them to the point where you could ask them to be your mentor.

Remember that you are 'God-made' and so pray every day for God's spirit to enhance, quicken and accelerate the gift.

The Battle of Entrepreneurship

It may be that as you read this book and particularly this chapter you are feeling pressured and stressed about work. Maybe your business is struggling. However you might describe it, right now, things just aren't adding up. I truly believe that Jesus can transform your work situation.

Jesus has shown that he is a business turn-around expert. The start of Jesus' public work was marked by a series of events that included his baptism, his testing by the devil and his declaration that, "The Spirit of the Lord is upon me." (Luke 4). He also came across a fisheries business 'Simon and Co.' the owner had been fishing all day and not caught a thing. This lack of a catch could have been going on for days or even weeks.

Jesus offered Simon and his team some advice, to put their nets down in deep water. Simon and Co. must have thought what on earth does a carpenter know about fishing. Given their lack of a catch they had nothing to lose so they put down their nets as advised. Simon and Co. caught such a large catch of fish that the nets came close to bursting. Simon called other local business owners to partner with them to share the catch and bring them to shore (Luke 5:1-11). If Jesus the carpenter can achieve a turn around with a fisheries business he can do so with any business, including yours.

A South African entrepreneur Francois van Niekerk founded a technology company in 1980 with less that R1,000 or £50 of start-up capital. Within nine months the business faced bankruptcy and in desperation Francois vowed that if Jesus turned the business around he would give 30% of the business to a foundation and give the money wherever God told him to. Within half an hour something happened that turned the situation around and the business was saved.

Francois followed through on his promise and placed 30% of the company's shares into an independent grant making trust, the Mergon Foundation. From these humble beginnings the Mergon Group of businesses has achieved above-market returns for nearly four decades. In response to Jesus' continued grace on the business, the van Niekerk family increased the Mergon Foundation's ownership of the business to 70% in 2008.

As well as helping businesses grow, Jesus can also cause businesses to struggle and economies to be disrupted. In the city of Ephesus there was a silversmith, Demetrius, who had developed a market for making imagines of Artemis. The apostle Paul had been preaching in the city that, "gods made by human hands are no gods at all." (Acts 19:26b) and there had been a powerful response. Demetrius called together the tradesmen and associated beneficiaries and created an uproar explaining that their business was at risk. Jesus can cause the downfall of business and the destabilising of whole economies.

Wealth and Super Wealthy

As I have mentioned wealth is a relative term. In common parlance wealth is defined as anyone who earns and owns more than you!

Every year *The Times* newspaper publishes its Rich List of Britain's richest. People skim read through the pages to see if any of their long lost relatives or school friends have made it big this year. I must say I always like to have a look through and see how many people I know and who the 'winners' and the 'losers' have been.

There is also a Global Rich List that puts things into perspective. Try putting your income into www.globalrichlist. com If you earn 25,000 pounds per annum you are in the top 1% of earners globally, if 100,000 pounds per annum you are in the top 0.07% of earners. Now that certainly changes your perspective on what it means to be wealthy, according to the Global Rich List many more of us fall into that category of wealthy than we might first have thought.

The World Wealth Report 2017, published by CapGemini defines High Net Worth Individuals, 'HNWI are those having investable assets worth more than USD $1 million or more, excluding primary residence, collectibles, consumables and consumer durables'. It reports that the HNWI population has grown by 7.5%, global HNWI wealth has grown by 8.2% and the fastest HNWI growing market for population is Russia at 20%. It also identifies the sectors that are perceived to produce the most millionaires by 2025:

- Financial Services 35.7%
- Technology and FinTech 30.9%
- Healthcare and Pharmaceuticals 30.1%
- Manufacturing 22.3%
- Real Estate and Construction 20.2%
- Communications 20.2%
- Education 19.8%
- Agriculture and Mining 18.9%
- Aerospace and Air Transportation 18%
- Renewable Energy 17%
- Entertainment and Recreation 15.2%
- Retail and Wholesale Trade 14%
- Transportation 13.9%
- Natural Resources 13.5%
- Utilities 6.6%
- Accommodation and Food Services 4%

The super wealthy never achieve their position through getting a job. You can probably tell by now that I'm not a big fan of limiting your income generation possibilities to getting a job or series of jobs over your life. It is entrepreneurship that creates wealth, or being in on the beginning of something big. It has been rumoured that the Initial Public Listing (IPO) on the stock markets of Facebook created more than a thousand millionaires.

Blessed for a Reason

God means for us to prosper holistically, however, he intends us to prosper for a reason. The Bible told Abraham that he was blessed to be a blessing, "I will make you into a great nation, and I will bless you; I will make your name great, and you will be a blessing." (Genesis 12:2). Too often, being blessed has become self-indulgent. A blessing has become reduced to an existential worship experience in which we cry out to God, 'more Lord, more!' Instead the true hallmark of being blessed is the blessing our lives are to humanity. We are blessed to be a blessing not blessed to be blessed.

The Bible talks about Israel as being a chosen nation, "Out of all the peoples on the face of the earth, the Lord has chosen you to be his treasured possession." (Deuteronomy 14:2). Israel, however, was not chosen to have an elite and exclusive relationship with God, Israel was chosen to be an example to all nations so that they would all worship God, "I will also make you a light for the Gentiles, that my salvation may reach to the ends of the earth." (Isaiah 49:6). Any privilege that we acquire is not for ourselves but for us to use in the benefit of others.

In the same way wealth creation is a gift from God not solely for the benefit of the entrepreneur but for the good of the world. Wealth creation can create jobs that lift families out of poverty rather than living on handouts from their family, charities or government. Wealth creation can build housing, schools, hospitals and businesses that regenerate whole communities. Wealth creation can drive the growth of economies and lift nations out of poverty and debt in a way that emergency aid and development never can.

I've just returned from lunch with the CEO of a fast growing company. The number of people it employs doubles every two years and it now employs more than 5,000 people. More than two-thirds of those employees are based in Eastern Europe where the employment is ensuring that families do not live in poverty and where the business is stimulating the economy. In this example and many others like it, the gift of wealth creation is being used to bless many.

There is a well-known international development charity, that has had its own problems recently, that regularly criticises wealthy people. It has said that the worlds richest eight billionaires, 'are as rich as the worlds poorest half, claiming that it is 'simply unacceptable'. What the charity fails to say is that five of the eight billionaires they criticise have committed themselves to The Giving Pledge to give away the majority of their wealth during their lifetime to combat poverty. We are blessed to be a blessing.

Wisdom about Wealth

The Bible is clear that there is absolutely nothing wrong with money and wealth creation, it is our attitude towards God and money that matters.

Solomon was the heir to the throne of the King of Israel. Despite the fact that he had been prepared for Kingship all his life when the day arrived he felt unprepared. So when God asked Solomon for anything he wanted he asked for wisdom and discernment to lead and govern the people of Israel. In response God said, "I will do what you have asked. I will give you a wise and discerning heart, so that there will never have been anyone like you, nor will there ever. Moreover, I will give you what you have not asked for – both wealth and honour – so that in your lifetime you will have no equal among kings" (1 Kings 3:12-13). God made Solomon the wealthiest king of his time, so God is certainly not against wealth but with great wealth comes great responsibility.

Thankfully, during Solomon's reign he wrote down the wisdom that God invested in his life which was brought together in the book of Proverbs. In many ways Proverbs is the first personal success book ever published.

Remembering God

We are all pretty forgetful particularly when it comes to what God does for us. There is a Biblical theme of remembering that occurs again and again because we have the tendency to forget.

When God gave Moses the ten commandments and in turn he passed them on to Israel he said, "Hear, O Israel: The Lord our God, the Lord is one. Love the Lord your God with all your heart and with all your soul and with all your strength. These commandments that I give you today are to be on your hearts. Impress them on your children. Talk about them when you sit at home and when you walk along the road, when you lie down and when you get up. Tie them as symbols on your hands and bind them on your foreheads. Write them on your houses and on your gates." (Deuteronomy 6:4-8). Our faith has many spiritual disciplines, traditions and habits and one of their objectives is to help us keep the main thing the main thing, to remember God in the mundane of each day as well as the remarkable.

When you begin generating wealth it is all too easy to take the credit, "it's because of my innovation, commerciality or hard work". We can claim we are 'self-made'. God had to remind his people, "But remember the Lord your God, for it is he who gives you the ability to produce wealth." (Deuteronomy 8:18). So never forget, especially if you become wealthy, remember that the ability to create wealth is a God-given gift. We are never self-made we are God-made. As Hannah the mother of the Prophet Samuel prayed, "The Lord makes poor and makes riches." (1 Samuel 2:7).

Finally, remember the God-given gift of wealth creation is only one gift of many that he can give to you. So if you haven't got that gift you will have others.

FREEDOM STEP 4

The fourth step towards financial freedom is to ask God for the gift of wealth creation because it is he who gives us the ability to produce wealth. God is the creator and he has made us in his image so we are creative.

A) Stop reading now and write a prayer asking God if he would give you the gift of wealth creation.

....

....

....

....

....

....

B) As with all gifts they become better as we start to exercise them. Record the practical steps you are going to take to begin to exercise the gift of wealth creation.

....

....

....

....

....

....

C) Given you cannot achieve success on your own, who are the people God has connected you to or is connecting you to in order to partner in business?

....

....

....

....

....

....

D) Write down exactly how you are going to use the blessing that God has given you to be a blessing to other people.

....

....

....

....

....

....

Step 5:
Develop multiple income streams

"Ship your grain across the sea; after many days you may receive a return. Invest in seven ventures, yes, in eight; you do not know what disaster may come upon the land. If clouds are full of water, they pour rain on the earth. Whether a tree falls to the south or to the north, in the place where it falls, there it will lie. Whoever watches the wind will not plant; whoever looks at the clouds will not reap. As you do not know the path of the wind, or how the body is formed in a mother's womb, so you cannot understand the work of God, the Maker of all things. Sow your seed in the morning, and at evening let your hands not be idle, for you do not know which will succeed, whether this or that, or whether both will do equally well."

Ecclesiastes 11:1-6

As I look back through my life to date, there have been many transitions, twists and turns. I pray every day that, 'I will live the great adventure of life in all its fullness with God' and God has certainly answered that prayer and led me in some great adventures. Some of my ventures have grown and flourished and others died before they had hardly begun.

There have been times when I have ended contracts with clients because I believed it was time to do something new. Common sense career advice would be to keep going with what you are doing even though you are unhappy in it, until you find what you are going to do next and then transition. I realise that's good advice but on occasions there is also a strength of conviction that it is time to change and you trust God to take a leap of faith without knowing what is going to emerge next.

On other occasions I've had the irresistible urge to start something that I really believed in. Sometimes that start-up has come to nothing and I've painfully lost all the money that I invested in the idea. On other occasions something that I thought would exist in the margins of my life has subsequently grown into a fully fledged international entity.

There have been times when my business has had no clients. Anyone who has worked as a freelancer or run their own business knows there are periods of 'feast and famine'. Times when you have way more than you need and times when you have way less than you need. The difference is, the famine normally preceeds the feast so there is no time to save up during the years of plenty! Those months and sometimes quarters when you have no clients are demoralising. It risks eroding your dignity and self-worth, and your motivation and get-up-and-go has just got up and gone somewhere else.

There have been a number of times when my wife and I made the decision to give up her income for us as a household because we were prioritising family. On the first occasion it was when we decided to start a family and at that point my wife was the main income earner for our household. Nearly a decade and three children later my wife returned to work,

God had provided incredibly during that season. On another occasion it was because we decided to homeschool one of our children because that was best for them. It wasn't a convenient time because we had just commissioned a large home improvement project but we stepped out in faith.

Having multiple income streams has given me the financial freedom to take leaps of faith, to take big risks in starting something new, to survive times of difficulty, to prioritise family life and much more besides. All this was possible because I have never relied on one income stream. I'm not saying that it has made it easy but with God it has made it possible. I am thankful that I have been able to follow God's spirit into whatever commercial, non-profit or family venture I believe he is calling me and long may it continue.

I am not suggesting that everyone should live this way or at this level of risk. What I do want to say is that anything is possible with God because he calls us to financial freedom to live life for Jesus without anxiety about money.

The Wisdom of Solomon

King Solomon the author of Ecclesiastes advises that you should have multiple ventures and income streams. His reasoning is that it makes you more resilient and sustainable through the different seasons of life and particularly through times of difficult adversity. He also explains that we do not know which of our ventures will succeed and which will not so we should diversify and spread the risk.

I have lost count of the number of entrepreneurs who said they 'lost everything' in the credit crunch of 2008. The reason being is they were so bullish in their belief that what they were invested in was going to continue to grow that they over exposed themselves. They highly geared their capital so that there was no wriggle room for a slight downturn let alone a market crash. They also chose to place all or the majority of their money in a single investment type rather than diversifying.

Vince Birley is the former Chief Strategy Officer of Ronald Blue one of the largest wealth management businesses serving Christian clients in the United States. Vince said that he works on the principle that no more than 5% should be invested into a single stock and no more than 7.5% in any one country. Its quite simple, financial diversification provides sustainability and resilience.

So if you are passionate about living your life for Jesus free from anxiety about money I would encourage you to develop seven or eight income streams. There are broadly four income generation models that I would like to propose for your consideration.

Employed

The first income model is that you have a job. Jobs are in many ways very attractive because they offer a level of security. You know how much you are going to get paid and how often. In addition to that you receive holiday pay, sick pay, maternity/paternity pay, as well as a pension and other benefits. There is a lot that can be said about the safe stability of a job which is why they are so popular.

On the downside a job generally means spending at least 40 hours a week for more than 40 years of your life working to earn just enough to survive and then retiring on 40% of what you could hardly afford to live on in the first place. Employment can result in a lifestyle that is about surviving from pay check to pay check.

Bishop Wayne Malcolm in his powerful book *The Miseducation of the Masses* critiques our current education system explaining that it educates and prepares people for a lifetime in a job rather than entrepreneurship and wealth creation. He explains that everything about the school system from set hours, bells, breaks, lunchtimes and management prepares children for a lifetime of servitude in a job. When you read his book you can't help but concur with his argument.

Personally I've never been a fan of having a job. I had one when I left school for five years and then I survived nicely without one for twenty-five years. I only have one now on a strictly part-time basis as part of a much wider work portfolio.

Self-Employed

The second income model is self-employment. Self-employment or freelancing is very appealing because of the freedom it offers. You can choose the hours you work, where you work them and take long weekends and holidays whenever you fancy. You know that in some years you may do extremely well and have bumper earnings that you use to do some special things with.

If being employed means that you have a job then to be self-employed means that a job owns you. As it turns out you don't choose what hours you work but rather your customers and clients do because you have to be available when they want you. It's the same with holidays, you end up fitting them in around quieter times of the year rather than when you might really like them. While there can be bumper years in terms of income there can also be times when your work struggles and your life becomes focused on the six-monthly tax bills. Consequently, being self-employed is often described as 'feast and famine'.

Personally I love being self-employed because I like the thrill and adventure and the faith and prayer that you need to exercise to get you through. I know this certainly doesn't suit everyone.

Business Owner

The third income model is business ownership. Business ownership is highly attractive because if it works well there is the potential for you to 'earn while you are asleep'. Fundamentally this is about owning a business system that does not require your constant attention and yet can produce a healthy profit. Then you can choose not just the hours you wish but whether you work in the traditional sense at all because you can appoint a managing director to run the business on your behalf.

As a business owner you can continue to draw a salary for your role as chair of the business and receive annual dividends based on business performance and profitability. Then at some point you can choose to sell the business and receive a nest egg payment for your next venture, a season of rest or whatever you choose to do next.

In many ways business ownership is the dream. The challenge is getting there. The majority of business start-ups fail within the first twelve-months. You never know whether your enterprise is going to be a winner or a loser until you've tried. Those businesses that make it require your blood, sweat and tears while you build them into something that can work without you. Only when your business can work without you have you really got a business that you can exit by selling to another interested party, and so most enterprises never make it that far. As discussed in the last chapter, wealth creation is a God-given gift so if it is something that we don't demonstratively have currently we can ask God for it.

Personally I love building something that can scale and operate without me although it really does ask absolutely everything from you on the route to getting there.

Investor

The fourth income model is that you become an investor and own shares in businesses. The big attraction of being an investor is that you find other people who are gifted wealth creators and they do the hard work of growing a business and your investment for you.

This of course is only possible when you have the cash to invest in the first place. You can generate that pot of cash to invest through the hard work of saving, realising some of the equity you may have in your home by remortgaging or the use of an inheritance.

There are numerous ways of investing. Over the years I've enjoyed investing in the start-up businesses of people I know which has resulted in me having shares in a variety of businesses including an artisan cheese monger, the album of a recording artist and a fintech company. These private investments have a high risk of failure, and it's also hard to get your money out once it's in. To encourage these types of investments Governments normally provide very attractive tax benefits to encourage investing.

Wealth management advice is increasingly becoming a combination of high-touch, i.e. deep client relationships and high-tech, i.e. online platforms and smartphone apps. The World Wealth Report 2017 explained that, 'Hybrid advice models are the future of wealth management' and, '54% of firms have hybrid-advice transformation underway but implementation is slow and ineffective'. While many of the established private bank and wealth management firms struggle with transformation there are technology driven market disrupters such as the MoneyTree and Nutmeg apps that are offering wealth investment advice at much lower charges.

Other investment disrupters include contentious cryptocurrencies such as Bitcoin and Ethereum. Those people who are advocates say that cryptocurrencies are the future because they are digital, global and transparent which means dislodging the 'middle man' i.e. banks. Others believe that cryptocurrencies are folly and nothing more than a digital pyramid scheme that will eventually collapse. The most basic of investment principles is to only invest what you can afford to lose, which becomes truer the more volatile the investment. I made a couple of short-term investments in Bitcoin and sold while it was on the up scooping an encouraging 50% return on investment, however, it was a high risk investment and so I only invested what I could afford to lose.

What is really important with investments is asset allocation. It's important to take King Solomons advice to diversify your portfolio and not put all your eggs in one basket. At the start of your career you may choose to be more of an adventurous pension investor to see what early growth can be achieved, however, as you approach retirement you would want to put your investments into much safer and stable assets.

Diversifying Income

These four income models are not mutually exclusive but rather a helpful way of thinking about how you can diversify your income portfolio as King Solomon advised.

So if you are employed don't give up your job. Instead you could develop an additional income stream alongside your job whether it is some self-employed freelance work, planning for a business start-up or developing your investment portfolio.

If you are a self-employed freelancer think about how you can transform what you do into a business system. In this way you can recruit and train other people to deliver the business with you and eventually perhaps for you.

If you are a business owner work towards your business system being delivered without you. This could include recruiting a managing director who can run the business on your behalf while you do the other things you want to do in life.

Whatever else you may be doing develop some investments. No matter how big or small the amount, make money work for you, not you for it. Put aside amounts of money every month and set aside lump sums when you have a windfall and start investing for the long-term.

Maybe you have got an aspect of each of these four models within your income portfolio and you are focused on growing them. The dream of course is to develop an income portfolio that does not require your constant attention but works on your behalf.

Where there is a Will

Generating additional income streams is something that everyone can do regardless of their starting point. Recently my family was doing a spring clean at home. The rooms in our house had become cluttered and the option of dumping things in the loft was no longer open to us because that was also cluttered and full. So we decided to fill our car with the things we no longer used and headed to our local car boot sale.

The people who turned up with a vehicle full of goods were either middle-class families like ourselves who were having an occasional clear out, trades people who turned up with vans full of knocked down retail goods or other families who did this week in week out in order to develop an additional income. As they say where there is a will there is a way!

This is what I call the 'car boot economy'. A cash sub-economy, buying, selling and trading that operates outside of high street shops and shopping centres, without involvement of banks and credit card companies. The families who do this week after week would be selling items from their home and restocking by purchasing goods from families like us who didn't really know what they were doing or what the things they were selling were worth.

Whatever your situation there are things you can do to supplement your income. As the saying goes, 'Necessity is the mother of invention' so when people need additional money and they have a strong work ethic they will find a way.

Branching Out

I have applied the Biblical principle of diversification to income but it can also be applied to savings. By diversifying our savings across different savings vehicles we increase their resilience to whatever might happen in the world around us.

Branching out spreads our risks and builds resilience in our financial fitness. It means that we can flourish and enjoy abundance in the good times and endure and survive during the difficult times. Sometimes those good and bad times are determined by our own decisions and sometimes because of factors outside our control but whatever happens you will be ready.

FREEDOM STEP 5

The fifth step to financial freedom is to develop multiple income streams so that during times of plenty you can live in abundance and during times of transition or difficulty you are resilient.

A) The Bible encourages us to have seven or eight income streams. Write down your current sources of income and how much each generates.

1] ....

2] ....

3] ....

4] ....

5] ....

6] ....

7] ....

8] ....

B) Estimate the percentage of your income that you receive from the following four types of income.

Employment ....

Self-employment/freelance ....

Business ownership ....

Investments ....

C) How financially resilient are you to the risk of losing your highest source or type of income?

Durable — Resistant — Stable — Vulnerable — Exposed

D) If you don't yet have seven or eight income streams what could you start doing today to develop an additional income stream/type in order to increase your resilience?

....

....

....

....

....

Step 6:
Spend less than you earn

"The wise store up choice food and olive oil,
but fools gulp theirs down."

Proverbs 21:20

When I was growing up my family wasn't poor, however, there certainly wasn't much spare money and there were long periods when money was a huge pressure. I remember not liking meat and that was nothing to do with wanting to be a vegetarian. The reason was that the cuts of meat my family could afford were mostly fat and bones so I grew up thinking I didn't like meat.

I also remember my mum sacrificially saving money each week from her housekeeping so that she could pay for me to go on the youth group weekend away. I'm not sure I appreciated what she did for me enough at the time but I am so grateful for all that she sacrificed to give my sister and I the best opportunities possible.

Other children at school talked about big and exciting birthday and Christmas presents, at that point I just kept quiet. They went on holiday to sunny beaches in Spain, to Disney in the US and other places that I could only dream of. They would talk about eating 'Chinese' or 'Indian' – I remember one day embarrassingly asking what they were talking about.

As a teenager I can remember getting excited because we were going out to a restaurant for the first time. I had no idea what to expect but I remember there was a famous American burger restaurant opening that everyone was talking about – it was McDonalds! Eating out was never part of our lifestyle.

My residing money memory from growing up was that our family couldn't afford stuff. We never talked about money as a family. Although I remember my mum and dad arguing about money in the kitchen while we watched TV in the other room or after we had gone to bed.

As a result when I started earning money I took the view that I would buy whatever I wanted whenever I wanted it. I became a spender, money was there to enjoy and I wasn't going to hold back. My dream was to drive a big four-by-four car, live in a mansion in the country and fly a helicopter into the city.

Number One

The single most important step to financial freedom is to spend less than you earn. In some ways I could have made this the very first step in this book, however, I decided it was important to establish the other steps as foundations first.

It's really pretty simple. If you spend more than you earn you will never have enough, you will acquire debt, and misery will follow. By comparison if you spend less than you earn you will always have enough, you will be free from debt and you will be far more likely to be happy. This is exactly what Charles Dickens wrote about in his book *David Copperfield* when one of the characters said, "Annual income twenty pounds, annual expenditure nineteen pounds nineteen shillings and six pence, result happiness. Annual income twenty pounds, annual expenditure twenty pounds ought and six, result misery."

This principle is so simple but we are so easily seduced to believe that we need to wear those clothes, drive that car or holiday in that destination. Our inner desire for more and better can take us to the edge of what we can really afford and in many cases over the edge of affordability.

When we spend more than we earn we become burdened by growing debt. We beat ourselves up, we don't sleep well and we snap at the people we love the most. Is it really worth it? What if we could be content to live on less than we earn? That is financial freedom.

Disciplined Budgeting

If you are going to spend less than you earn you need to find a way of living with a margin of surplus between your income and expenditure. Again this is not about how much money you have. People can have a lot of money but still be miserable because they spend more than they have.

Not many people can achieve an underspend intuitively, most people need a budget that is written down in order to be able to achieve that target.

A budget begins with calculating all the ways that you generate an income so that you know what you are working with. As explored in the previous chapter this could be from employment, self-employment, business ownership and investments. You might have a single income source or you might have seven or eight as suggested by the wisdom of Solomon.

The first principle of budgeting is that you give to God first. As the apostle Paul advises the church in the city of Corinth, "On the first day of every week, each one of you should set aside a sum of money in keeping with your income, saving it up, so that when I come no collections will have to be made." (1 Corinthians 16:2). While recognising we live under grace many people choose to follow the Old Testament principle of the tithe and give the first ten percent of what they earn. We will explore giving much more in 'Step 8: Reflect God through your generosity'.

The second principle of budgeting is to set aside some money just in case or as the saying goes money for a 'rainy day' – when things may not be as good. Joseph interpreted the Pharaoh's dreams explaining that there would be seven years of abundant harvest and seven years of famine. He recommended that a fifth of the harvest be saved during the seven years of plenty so that during the seven years of austerity all would be well (Genesis 41:34). This is basically 'rainy day' planning to set aside 20% of what you earn today for when you may face difficult days in the future.

The third principle of budgeting is spend less that you earn. As King Solomon's proverb quoted at the start of the chapter says, "The wise store up choice food and olive oil, but fools gulp theirs down." (Proverbs 21:20). Only foolish people consume all they have, the wise take care about how much they use. King Solomon sees an example in the life of an ant! He says, "Go the ant, you sluggard; consider its ways and be wise! It has not commander, no overseer or ruler, yet it stores its provisions in summer and gathers its food at harvest." (Proverbs 6:6-8). Simply put, if an ant can do it how much more should we.

There are three main types of expenditure that go into a budget: a) fixed expenses, e.g. rent or mortgage, utility bills and council tax, b) variable expenses, e.g. food shopping, clothes and entertainment, and c) periodic expenses, e.g. holidays, car insurance and gifts. The peaks and troughs of periodic costs can be difficult to budget so I try and move as many items from annual to monthly payments as possible. For example car insurance can be paid in one annual fee or split over 12 months often without additional charge, and holiday costs can either fall in the month you take the holiday or you can set aside money every month for your annual holiday.

When it comes to budgeting you can't beat a good old fashioned spreadsheet to map out how much money you are going to spend on what. There are also a number of smart phone apps that can help you budget and keep track of what you have spent and how much you have left.

One of the keys to budgeting, to spend less than you earn, is to understand the difference between needs and wants. It is so easy to dress up wants as needs. If we are really honest with ourselves most of the things we think we need are really wants and if we really needed to we could make do without them.

It's all about planning what you are going to do with your money before you get your hands on it. Once it gets into your hands and you don't have a plan anything can happen. Good financial disciplines like budgeting create incredible financial freedom.

Marriage Budgeting

When you are married, budgeting becomes more complicated. You and your spouse will have probably had different experiences of money growing up and have developed different financial personalities. As mentioned my financial personality is a spender because of my upbringing and my wife has the financial personality of a saver because of her upbringing and so we have to be careful. If Esther saves our money and I spend our money she would rightly become resentful pretty quickly.

As with most marriage 'issues', being tender hearted and effective communication is always a significant part of the solution. When Esther and I were first married we had an agreement that if we wanted to spend more than a certain amount of money, we would ask each other's permission. This worked really well and then the agreement became history, however, it has become our culture and ingrained habit to talk with each other about large purchases.

When it comes to money, couples can have different views on how much to give, how much to save, about investment risks and a myriad of other money matters. The only root through is good communication, together with the compromise of your own preferences. Never confuse the compromise of strongly held preferences with the compromise of strongly held values, they are not the same thing. People are often rigid about strongly help preferences whereas we should flex these to make room for healthy relationships in our lives.

When Esther and I discuss how we will balance our budget we have different responses, as with most things in our marriage. Esther looks at how we can spend less and I always look at where we can earn more. Two are always better than one, both of these strategies are important to balance the household budget both to reduce expenditure and increase income,

Our (read Esther's) favourite ways of reducing expenditure are: serve in the community more and mooch online and in the high street shops less, shop at a cheaper supermarket, cook at home more and go out for dinner and order takeaways less, make do and mend with the clothes you have and change your utility providers in order to get a better offer.

Our (read Matt's) favourite ways of increasing income are: make more new business telephone calls, write and publish a new book, put a lodger in the guest room (which in the UK benefits from attractive tax relief) or take an international business trip to generate new opportunities and revenue.

Creating a balanced budget is not easy especially when there is more than one person who is spending money but it's critical that you do, to avoid debt and misery.

Healthy Debt

In living by the principle of spending less than you earn, understanding what is healthy and what is crippling about debt is extremely important.

I once met a rather naive Christian who believed that debt was wrong and therefore you shouldn't have a mortgage to buy a home. Their idealism lasted for as long as they didn't need to buy a home, and when they needed a home for their family all of a sudden their theology changed. I tell this story not to mock them but to say that there is debt that is crippling and out of control and there is debt in the form of a structured loan that can be liberating and managed such as a mortgage to buy a home.

The Bible clearly does not forbid debt otherwise it would not give guidelines about lending and repaying. The apostle Paul says to the Romans, "Give to everyone what you owe them: If you owe taxes, pay taxes; if revenue, then revenue; if respect, then respect; if honor, then honor. Let no debt remain outstanding." (Romans 13:8). The advice is obvious but the practice is so often inconsistently applied.

The Bible also recognises that debt enslaves us, "The rich rule over the poor, and the borrower is slave to the lender." (Proverbs 22:7). However, we are made to be enslaved to no one but Jesus. If you do spend more than you earn the result will be debt and it's best to get out of debt as soon as possible.

Crippling Debt

Debt can be crippling. It can have a negative impact upon our peace of mind, our well-being and health and, as we come back to time and time again, our ability to live life with freedom from concern about money to follow Jesus. If you are in debt or have ever been in debt you will know this all too well.

We live in a world that spends more than it earns. In 2017, UK Government debt stood at £1.7 trillion, equivalent to 88% of GDP and household debt, including mortgages, credit cards and student loans was £1.6 trillion (Source: Bank of England). In 2017, US Government debt was around $20 trillion, equivalent to more than 100% of GDP and household dept, including mortgages, student loans, car loans and credit cards was $12.7 trillion (Source: Federal Reserve Bank of New York).

The UK Financial Conduct Authority 'Financial Lives' 2017 survey showed that 4.1 million adults are in serious financial difficulty. Seventeen per cent of adults were shown to be in financial vulnerability, because if their monthly bills increased by £50 they would struggle. When you are in strained financial circumstances it is difficult if not impossible to live out your God-given purpose because you are focused on financial survival.

Michael Jackson died at 50 years old having sold 61million albums and yet owing $500 million. Since he died and stopped spending, the executors of his estate have made decisions that have turned that debt into a profit. It does not matter how much you earn it's whether you spend less than you earn that determines whether you are financially free or not.

Freedom from Debt

If you are in debt and want to become financially free then act immediately. Find someone who handles money well and ask for their advice, just having someone who can both support you and hold you to account will be a massive help.

Move to a cash economy and only spend money that you have. This will mean cutting up your credit cards so that the temptation to spend more than you earn is completely removed. Then stop all non-essential spending. Try to eliminate periodic costs and reduce variable expenses to as little as possible.

Map out all your debts and how much interest you are paying on each. Then begin by focusing on repaying debts with the highest levels of compound interest first. Speak to the companies you owe the money to. Discuss and agree a repayment plan. Consolidate your debts and simplify them wherever possible. Develop an immediate action plan to get yourself back on track.

Financial Liberation

Spending less than you earn is incredibly liberating. It actually doesn't matter how little or how much you earn. As long as you spend less than you earn, you have the potential to be happy. If, however, you spend more than you earn you will be miserable.

FREEDOM STEP 6

The sixth step to financial freedom is to spend less than you earn.

A) Calculate your total income and total expenditure (whether weekly, monthly or annually). Are you spending more than you earn or less than you earn? If you find yourself trying hard to make the figures balance it is more likely that you are spending more than you earn.

Total Earnings ....

Total Expenditure ....

Balance ....

Are you spending MORE or LESS than you earn? ....

B) Spending more than you earn means that you are unable to live life for Jesus free from concern about money. If this is the case are you willing to commit to taking immediate action?

Yes or No

C) What three things can you do immediately to start reducing your expenditure?

1] ....

2] ....

3] ....

D) What three things can you do immediately to start increasing your income?

1] ....

2] ....

3] ....

E) Create a budget for yourself. I use a spreadsheet with months along the horizontal and 'income' and 'expenditure' on the vertical with an auto calculating 'balance' at the top.

Include all your income types; employment income, self-employment income, business ownership income and investment income.

Then add your expenditure; giving, 'rainy day' saving, future saving, fixed expenses, e.g. rent/mortgage, variable expenses e.g. food and clothes and periodic expenses e.g. car service and holidays.

If following this budget will enable you to live with a margin of underspend then stick to it If not what variable expenses and periodic expenses can you reduce or stop? Or how can you create more income?

....

....

....

Step 7:
Put your money to work

"At that time the kingdom of heaven will be like... Again, it will be like a man going on a journey, who called his servants and entrusted his wealth to them. To one he gave five bags of gold, to another two bags, and to another one bag, each according to his ability. Then he went on his journey. The man who had received five bags of gold went at once and put his money to work and gained five bags more. So also, the one with two bags of gold gained two more. But the man who had received one bag went off, dug a hole in the ground and hid his master's money. After a long time the master of those servants returned and settled accounts with them. The man who had received five bags of gold brought the other five. 'Master,' he said, 'you entrusted me with five bags of gold. See, I have gained five more.' His master replied, 'Well done, good and faithful servant! You have been faithful with a few things; I will put you in charge of many things. Come and share your master's happiness!' The man with two bags of gold also came. 'Master,' he said, 'you entrusted me with two bags of gold; see, I have gained two more.' His master replied, 'Well done, good and faithful servant! You have been faithful with a few things; I will put you in charge of many things. Come and share your master's happiness!' Then the man who had received one bag of gold came. 'Master,' he said, 'I knew that you are a hard man, harvesting where you have not sown and gathering where you have not scattered seed. So I was afraid and went out and hid your gold in the ground. See, here is what belongs to you.' His master replied, 'You wicked, lazy servant! So you knew that I harvest where I have not sown and

gather where I have not scattered seed? Well then, you should have put my money on deposit with the bankers, so that when I returned I would have received it back with interest. "So take the bag of gold from him and give it to the one who has ten bags. For whoever has will be given more, and they will have an abundance. Whoever does not have, even what they have will be taken from them. And throw that worthless servant outside, into the darkness, where there will be weeping and gnashing of teeth."

Matthew 25:1a & 14-30

'A lemonade income but a champagne lifestyle' is the way my close friends used to describe me. I didn't used to earn very much but I certainly knew how to spend it having a good time.

I take the words of Jesus very seriously when he says, "I have come that they may have life, and have it to the full." (John 10:10b). The daily office (set of prayers) that I have written and say everyday includes a line asking, 'Help me live the great adventure of life in all its fullness with God.' This isn't only a nice scripture and a nice prayer it is something I live with every ounce of my being. I believe God wants us to make the most of every moment and live life to the absolute maximum of its potential.

As I described earlier in this book my historic financial personality is a spender. During my growing-up years there was a lack of money which I really really resented. So when I started earning a living for myself I started making up for what I viewed as a poverty lifestyle growing up. I would buy whatever I wanted as soon as I wanted it. Shopping was a fun hobby.

Later in life God challenged me. God didn't challenge me about having a good time he loves it when we live life to the maximum. What he challenged me about was my financial decisions. I realised that virtually all the financial decisions I was making were about the short-term here and now spending. Virtually none of my financial choices were about the medium or long-term. In my passion to avoid a poverty existence I had inadvertently walked into another trap of making poor financial choices by blowing everything whenever I got it.

It was then that I realised I needed to be making more medium and long-term financial decisions. I started saving money on a monthly basis in a tax efficient investment vehicle. I committed to making a series of highly tax efficient investments into business start-ups. Even though I'm uncertain about the concept of 'retirement' I optimised the tax benefits of saving into a pension fund by increasing my monthly contributions. I will always have a default inclination to spend rather than save and so building in disciplines like these is really important to combat my instincts.

Other people have the opposite challenge to me. They are so concerned with saving and protecting the money they earn for the future that they live a 'half-life'. Some will buy a home that is a 'property project' and having developed it never furnish it so they can enjoy it with family, friends and strangers alike. Some choose to live in patched up old clothes when they could easily buy themselves a new 'wardrobe'. Some never go on a decent holiday and yet have money piled up in the bank. There is nothing wrong with being frugal but I think there is something wrong with being stingy with ourselves and others. That balance is going to look different for different people.

Be Trustworthy

Jesus explains that the kingdom of heaven is like the man who rewards people who put money to work but penalises people who do nothing with what he has entrusted to them (Matthew 25:14-30). Jesus expects us to put to work the talents he has given us in order to produce a return for him. It seems from this story that Jesus rewards people who take risks and steps of faith into the unknown and penalises people who demonstrate excessive caution and a lack of faith. He also makes clear that there are rewards to come for those who are faithful with what he entrusts to them now.

Jesus said that the very least we should do is to put money on deposit at the bank so that it produces interest (Matthew 25:27). There is, however, clear expectation that we will do way more than put money on deposit and produce some interest. We can invest in one of our own ventures or somebody else's and potentially receive a far higher rate of return.

In another money story that Jesus told his disciples he said,

"There was a rich man whose manager was accused of wasting his possessions. So he called him in and asked him, 'What is this I hear about you? Give an account of your management, because you cannot be manager any longer.' The manager said to himself, 'What shall I do now? My master is taking away my job. I'm not strong enough to dig, and I'm ashamed to beg... I know what I'll do so that, when I lose my job here, people will welcome me into their houses.' So he called in each one of his master's debtors. He asked the first, 'How much do you owe my master?' 'Nine hundred gallons of olive oil,' he replied. The manager told him, 'Take your bill, sit down quickly, and make it four hundred and fifty.' Then he asked the second, 'And how much do you owe?' ' 'A thousand bushels of wheat,' he replied. He told him, 'Take your bill and make it eight hundred.' The master commended the dishonest manager because he had acted shrewdly. For the people of this world are more shrewd in dealing with their own kind than are the people of the light. I tell you, use worldly wealth to gain friends for yourselves, so that when it is gone, you will be welcomed into eternal dwellings. Whoever can be trusted with very little can also be trusted with much, and whoever is dishonest with very little will also be dishonest with much. So if you have not been trustworthy in handling worldly wealth, who will trust you with true riches? And if you have not been trustworthy with someone else's property, who will give you property of your own? No one can serve two masters. Either you will hate the one and love the other, or you will be devoted to the one and despise the other. You cannot serve both God and money." The Pharisees, who loved money, heard all this and were sneering at Jesus. He said to them, 'You are the ones who justify yourselves in the eyes of others, but God knows your hearts. What people value highly is detestable in God's sight.'" (Luke 16:1-14).

The story portrays God as someone who rewards people who are wise and shrewd with money. It makes clear that if your prove yourself to be trustworthy with small amounts of money God will entrust you with larger amounts of money. Depending on your political and economic leanings this text could make you feel uncomfortable but there is no escaping that it is Biblical.

Compound Interest

When Jerusalem lay in ruins and God's people were working to rebuild it, Nehemiah challenged the Jewish aristocracy not to charge their own people interest on loans. The interest was becoming a crippling burden on God's people. The taxes payable to the King combined with the loans and interest was becoming so great that the people were being driven to enslave their sons and daughters. Nehemiah said, "You are charging your own people interest!... What you are doing is not right... But let us stop charging interest." (Nehemiah 5:7b, 9a, 10b). The Jewish aristocracy responded positively saying, "We will give it back... and we will not demand anything more from them. We will do as you say." (Nehemiah 5:12). In some situations interest and compound interest can mean that we lose our financial freedom.

When associated with debt for example compound interest is the interest that is payable not only on the initial debt but also on subsequent interest charged which if not repaid results in debt growing exponentially. If you were to have a credit card debt of $7,500.00 with an APR of 29.99% compounded daily (as credit cards are) then after a year you will owe $10,122.70. Just imagine how fast that debt could spiral out of control if left unpaid.

The Rule of 72

Compound interest when applied to money on deposit can create significant growth over time. Your initial deposit grows according to the rate of interest but in year two you not only receive interest on the initial deposit but also on the interest you received in year one.

There is a finance principle that estimates how long it takes to double your money. It is called 'The Rule of 72' and explains that when you divide the annual rate of interest expressed as a percentage into the 72, it will produce the number of years to double your investment.

So a deposit benefiting from 1% interest would take 72 years to double, at 2% would take 36 years, at 4% would take 18 years, at 8% would take 9 years. So $10,000 benefiting from 8% interest would take 9 years to grow into $20,000.

The rule of 72 is a reasonably accurate estimate for interest rates between 6% and 10%. When dealing with interest rates outside of this range, the rule can be adjusted by subtracting or adding 1 from 72 for every 3% points. So for 5% the rule is adjusted to 71 and for 14% the rule is adjusted to 74.

You may feel like you are too broke to make money work for you. I completely understand being in that place. You simply feel like you haven't got enough to do the basics let alone save. I would encourage you to consider saving a small amount. Imagine the satisfaction of saving an amount of money over a number years and seeing that amount double.

The risk of saying you will save when times are better is that those better times never come and so you never end up saving. So make a start with an amount no matter how small and seemingly insignificant.

Invest Wisely

The prophet Jeremiah had a difficult job. He was sent to God's people to warn them that because of their unfaithfulness to other god's that they would be punished. "The Lord Almighty, who planted you, has decreed disaster for you, because the people of both Israel and Judah have done evil and aroused my anger by burning incense to Baal.' (Jeremiah 11:17) and "You have rejected me," declares the Lord. "You keep on backsliding. So I will reach out and destroy you; I am tired of holding back." (Jeremiah 15:6). For most of his working life Jeremiah was a real gloom and doom merchant.

Then Israel was under siege from the Babylonians and Jeremiah's message switched to a message of hope that they would one day return to the land. God told Jeremiah to buy land in Israel that would soon come under Babylonian rule. Jeremiah said, "The word of the Lord came to me: Hanamel son of Shallum your uncle is going to come to you and say, 'Buy my field at Anathoth, because as nearest relative, it is your right and duty to buy it.'" (Jeremiah 32:6-7). From a human perspective this was a pretty unwise investment. He was to take ownership of land that would be plundered and occupied by the Babylonians.

"This is what the Lord says: 'As I have brought all this great calamity on this people, so I will give them all the prosperity

I have promised them. Once more fields will be bought in this land of which you say, "It is a desolate waste, without people or animals, for it has been given into the hands of the Babylonians." Fields will be bought for silver, and deeds will be signed, sealed and witnessed in the territory of Benjamin, in the villages around Jerusalem, in the towns of Judah and in the towns of the hill country, of the western foothills and of the Negev, because I will restore their fortunes,' declares the Lord." (Jeremiah 32:42-44). Jeremiah believed that God had spoken to him and that the investment in buying the field would be a good one because one day the people of Israel would return to their land.

So the field Jeremiah purchased was actually a very wise investment decision. The value of the field just prior to Babylonian occupation must have been at rock bottom. By the time God returned Israel and restored their fortunes the field would be far more valuable. As the wise invest advice says, 'buy low and sell high'.

Working for Money?

Most people work for money rather than have money work for them. Having money work for you through a portfolio or savings and investments is very liberating and is another step towards financial freedom. So start making financial decisions that are about the long-term.

FREEDOM STEP 7

The seventh step to financial freedom is to make money work for your rather than you working for money.

A) How much money per month could you afford to start putting aside to make it work for you?

....

B) If you cut back on some expenditure how much more money could you afford to put aside to start working for you?

....

C) If you increased your income how much more money could you afford to put aside to start working for you?

....

D) What are the most tax-efficient ways available within your country to start making money work for you?

....

....

....

E) What trustworthy professional could you go to for financial advice?

....

....

....

Step 8:
Reflect God through your generosity

"For the kingdom of heaven is like a landowner who went out early in the morning to hire workers for his vineyard. He agreed to pay them a denarius for the day and sent them into his vineyard. About nine in the morning he went out and saw others standing in the marketplace doing nothing. He told them, 'You also go and work in my vineyard, and I will pay you whatever is right.' So they went. He went out again about noon and about three in the afternoon and did the same thing. About five in the afternoon he went out and found still others standing around. He asked them, 'Why have you been standing here all day long doing nothing?' 'Because no one has hired us,' they answered. He said to them, 'You also go and work in my vineyard.' When evening came, the owner of the vineyard said to his foreman, 'Call the workers and pay them their wages, beginning with the last ones hired and going on to the first.' The workers who were hired about five in the afternoon came and each received a denarius. So when those came who were hired first, they expected to receive more. But each one of them also received a denarius. When they received it, they began to grumble against the landowner. 'These who were hired last worked only one hour,' they said, 'and you have made them equal to us who have borne the burden of the work and the heat of the day.' But he answered one of them, 'I am not being unfair to you, friend. Didn't you agree to work for a denarius? Take your pay and go. I want to give the one who was hired last the same as I gave you. Don't I have the right to do what I want with my own money? Or are you envious because I am generous?"

Matthew 20:1-15

Reality television is the broadcast genre of our generation. Whether you love outdoor survival, luxury island holidays, baking the best cakes, driving the fastest cars, buying and developing residential properties, discovering the latest recording artist, learning to ballroom dance or even dance on ice there is a reality television show for you. One of my favourites is *Dragon's Den* (UK) or *Shark Tank* (US) where people who have a business start-up present to a group of entrepreneurial business investors asking for capital and assistance to grow their business to the next level.

Inspired by *Dragon's Den* and *Shark Tank* I've created a philanthropic approach through which churches and charities can pitch for support and generous people can give towards those causes. It is so exciting to see 50 philanthropists gather to hear carefully selected non-profits pitch for the resources to scale their approach to social transformation. After each pitch the gathered audience has the opportunity to ask any question they wish of the project and then at the end of the evening to donate to one, or more, or all of the gathered projects.

In slightly different formats and with a variety of partners and clients I have now run more than 25 of these *Dragons Den* or *Shark Tank* style events. I have seen the audiences give more than £2 million. Having undertaken an evaluation of recipients of this funding the key finding was that, while the generosity of the money they received was significant, it was the people they met that was more valuable. The generous ways in which people helped them write a business plan, join their boards and make introductions was what made the greatest difference to the growth of their projects.

Generosity

One of my favourite stories that Jesus told is of the landowner who went out early one morning to hire workers for his vineyard. That year must have been a bumper harvest because throughout the the the day the owner of the vineyard hired more workers to ensure that the harvest was brought in successfully. At the end of the day the workers were surprised that those who were hired last were paid the same as the workers who were hired first. Even though the workers who were hired first were paid what was agreed they were furious that those who worked less were paid exactly the same. You can imagine the workers calling in the unions and threatening to strike. Then the landowner said to the people that he had hired, "Are you envious because I am generous?"

The truth is that God treats us all as we don't deserve – he is generous! None of us deserve the generosity of God and yet he is generous anyway. This is the heart of the gospel of Jesus Christ, that we are saved by grace. The way on in our faith is the same as the way into our faith, it's by grace. We are made righteous not by our own efforts but by God's grace and generosity.

We are invited by Jesus to love others as he has loved us and that isn't easy because the way that he has loved us is so generous. We are invited by Jesus to love others regardless of whether they love us in return. That is the most generous and extravagant love. It's not just a generosity with our money but it's generosity with our lives. As we explored it's about giving our talent, time and trust as well as our treasure. In this chapter we shall focus on generosity with our treasure.

Giving

A few years ago the BBC undertook research about financial generosity. One of the findings was that Christians are more generous than people who are not Christians. The BBC asked if I would be willing to be interviewed on twenty regional radios stations about the research.

The big risk was that the research could be presented or understood as Christians being better than other people. So I decided that my key message would be that people who follow Jesus are not better than others, they are simply trying to reflect the generosity of the God that they follow.

Giving is not about tithing 10%. It's not about developing a sophisticated system of giving based on Old Testament thinking and models of tithes and offerings. Giving is an expression of the generous heart of God.

Gleanings

The Bible has so many different teachings, pictures and stories about generous giving.

Leviticus (19:9-10) says to farmers, "When you reap the harvest of your land, do not reap to the very edges of your field or gather the gleanings of your harvest," and to vineyard owners, "Do not go over your vineyard a second time or pick up the grapes that have fallen. Instead, leave them for the poor and the foreigner." Modern viticulture often does more than one sweep of the vines to harvest the fruit at exactly the right time – the Bible is certainly not rebuking this. The Biblical principle is that whatever business we are in we are not to take all the spoils for ourselves but to be generous and ensure that those who have nothing or very little are looked after.

The story of Naomi is a sad one, her husband dies and so do her sons and so she sends her two daughters-in-law home to their families. One of them, Ruth refuses to abandon her mother-in-law and so they live by faith. Ruth says to Naomi, "Let me go to the fields and pick up the left over grain behind anyone in whose eyes I find favor." (Ruth 2:2). This is Naomi and Ruth living off of the gleanings of the farmers.

Jubilee

The Bible also teaches the year of Jubilee which is a special year of generosity, "Consecrate the fiftieth year and proclaim liberty throughout the land to all its inhabitants. It shall be a Jubilee for you; each of you is to return to your family property and to your own clan." (Lev25:10). As you read on through the twenty-fifth chapter of Leviticus there are all sorts of instructions about what to do and not do during Jubilee.

Despite this, there is no evidence within the Bible or other historical documents that Jubilee was ever practiced. There are, however, people who have marked a jubilee year in different ways. I know one couple who in their 50th birthday year gave away 100% of what they earned. What an incredible privilege to prayerfully give away your year's earnings.

Tithe

Then there is the tithe which the Old Testament teaches is the first 10% of what you earn that is given to God, "A tithe of everything from the land, whether grain from the soil or fruit from the trees, belongs to the Lord; it is holy to the Lord." (Lev27:30). Jesus doesn't teach about tithing, although as a good Jew you can't imagine that he was loyal to the practice. In one of his rants against religious leaders, Jesus does reference the tithe when he says, "You give a tenth of your spices – mint, dill and cumin. But you have neglected the more important matters of the law – justice, mercy and faithfulness. You should have practiced the latter, with neglecting the former." (Matthew 23:23).

Personally I practice tithing. For me it is not about giving God what belongs to him, giving a tithe is a declaration that everything I have and everything I am belongs to him. It's always good to remember that God doesn't need our money but he does want us!

Mite

I love the story of the 'widows mite' (an old world for coin) or how it is increasingly known 'widows offering', "Jesus sat down opposite the place where the offerings were put and watched the crowd putting their money into the temple treasury. Many rich people threw in large amounts. But a poor widow came and put in two very small copper coins, worth only a few cents." (Mark 12:43). Jesus drew together his disciples and said, "Truly I tell you, this poor widow has put more into the treasury than all the others. They all gave out of their wealth; but she, out of her poverty, put in everything – all she had to live on." (Mark 12:44). It is clear from this story that it is not about how much we give but how much of ourselves we are giving in our generosity.

Travelling to the poorest communities in the world, whether in slums, townships, favelas, streets or rural areas, is overwhelming because of their generosity. People who have very very little are often some of the most generous people in the world. On a family adventure in India we visited a street community in Mumbai. We never forget seeing small children asleep on the pavement with a single blanket under them and a sheet of plastic above them. On the wall beside them a plastic carrier bag hung on nail, the bag contained all that that family owned. We visited the 'pavement school' where local volunteers provided learning experiences for the children. One of the most humbling experiences of our lives is when we were given fresh bouquets of flowers by the families. Those flowers are now dried and hang in our kitchen to remind us what real generosity looks like.

Five Loaves

One day a huge crowd began to follow Jesus and his concern was how they were going to feed so many people. Then a young boy came forward with five small barley loaves and two fish and the disciples said to Jesus, "…how far will they go among so many?" (John 6:8). Jesus gave thanks for the loaves and fish and the crowd was fed, in fact what was left, "filled twelve baskets with the pieces of barley loads left over by those who had eaten." (John 6:13).

This is classic God. When we offer our little, God achieves so much. Then after the job is done there is an abundance left. This is what the Kingdom of God looks like.

Hospitality

When the apostle Paul visited the city of Philippi he visited the river and met some women who he spoke to about Jesus. The Bible tells us that "One of those listening was a woman from the city of Thyatira named Lydia, a dealer in purple cloth." (Acts16:14). Lydia believed what she heard and so she was baptised and then insisted that Paul and his team, "come and stay at my house" (Acts 16:15). As soon as Lydia believed her instinct was to give through hospitality.

Recently my family and I were taking a road trip around California. We stayed in hotels, motels, lodges and in homes. Each morning my children would ask, "where are we staying tonight?" On one occasion I explained we were going to stay in a home of a man I had had a ten minute conversation with and so I didn't know much about them. It led to a really interesting discussion about showing hospitality to strangers and virtual strangers.

The conversation reminded me of Henri Nouwen's book *Reaching Out* and one of the sections that is called 'Hostility to hospitality'. Growing up, and for good reason, we were all taught not to talk to strangers which is rather sad because often that carries on into adult life. The world around us is often unwelcoming and hostile rather than inviting and hospitable to strangers.

Giving Stories

There are so many teachings, stories and models about generous giving and living in the Bible, and in today's church which can inspire us in how we give.

An American couple I know have given 100% of the ownership of their business into a grant making foundation. They have personally chosen to live on the same salary that they received when they first started out in the business. They live in the same house, they drive a small car and live a modest Western lifestyle. The foundation now hires more than 80 people to ensure that the tens of millions of dollars that is given away every year is given away well.

An English family do something similar but slightly different. Each year they review how much money they believe God wants them to live on. Then whatever their business earns above that figure they choose to give away.

Another family business meet together on on a monthly basis to discuss, pray and agree together how they will give away their money. I met the son the day before he was going off to his families giving day and he explained how it was one of the most enjoyable days of his month.

There is a UK businessman who believes that God blessed him so much that he has worked his way to a place where he 'reverse tithes'. Instead of giving 10% of his earning to God and living on 90% he now gives to God 90% of what he earns and lives on 10%.

I remember hosting a private dinner for a father and son to talk about how they gave generously. The father explained that his experience is that the more money he gave to God the more money he made, in his own words he said, "You can't out give God. God's spade is much bigger than ours."

There are so many creative and enjoyable ways that you can reflect God through your generosity. Of course a tithe is good but there are many other possibilities beyond a straight 10%.

FREEDOM STEP 8

The eighth step to financial freedom is to reflect the character of God through your generosity.

A) What Biblical story of giving most inspires you?

....

....

B) What contemporary story of giving most inspires you by reflecting the character of God?

....

....

C) When you look back over your life to date what has your giving story been?

....

....

....

D) Looking to the life ahead of you what would you like your giving story to be?

....

....

....

E) What action can you take today, this week and this month to ensure you are taking steps towards realising the giving story you want to have?

Today ....

This week ....

This month ....

Step 9:
Plan for your future

"Suppose one of you wants to build a tower. Won't you first sit down and estimate the cost to see if you have enough money to complete it? For if you lay the foundation and are not able to finish it, everyone who sees it will ridicule you, saying, 'This person began to build and wasn't able to finish.' Or suppose a king is about to go to war against another king. Won't he first sit down and consider whether he is able with ten thousand men to oppose the one coming against him with twenty thousand? If he is not able, he will send a delegation while the other is still a long way off and will ask for terms of peace. In the same way, those of you who do not give up everything you have cannot be my disciples."

Luke 14:28-33

The church family weekend had been a fantastic time away. We were now on our way home in a car far less carefully packed than it had been on the way there. A conversation started amongst our family about what we had enjoyed most about the weekend. I loved the countryside walk in my wellington boots and coming back to sit in front of the log fire to defrost with a warming drink. My wife had enjoyed the conversations with people she doesn't normally get the opportunity to talk with and also the worship and Bible study.

The children talked about entertainment night and the fun and games they had with friends, however, what they enjoyed the most was the indoor heated swimming pool. They had swum in it morning, noon and night every day and were developing permanent water wrinkles.

The children began to talk about how much they would like a swimming pool at home. I interjected pretty quickly to explain the expense of the installation and maintenance of a swimming pool and that if they really wanted one they would be wise to start saving for one sooner rather than later.

I suggested that we get each of our three children extra piggy banks so they had three each; one for spending, another for saving and a third for sharing with other people. Then each week I would ensure that their pocket money contained a minimum of three coins so they had something to put in each piggy bank. The rules were twofold. Firstly, that they had to put some money in each piggy bank each week but exactly how much was their choice and secondly, that they could not move money out of saving and sharing into spending.

Years later when our children receive their pocket money they continue to put some aside for saving and sharing as well as spending. Although they now receive their pocket money electronically into a bank account with a special children's debit card, they have set up regular weekly payments into their saving and sharing allocations.

Some time later I learnt that Jewish children are taught to manage their money in five jars. The first jar is for their tithe or 10% to God, the second jar is for 10% to charity, the third is 10% to save for an emergency, a fourth jar 20% to invest and benefit from compound interest and the fifth jar is 50% for spending. Perhaps this diligence and discipline with money is part of the explanation why Jewish people are renowned for their resourcefulness and wealth.

Planning for the future is something that you are hardly ever too young to start and never too old to begin.

Planning

Jesus encourages us to count the cost of things before we start them. He explains that we would be foolish to start a building project without first sitting down and working out a budget. Again Jesus illustrates by explaining that you would be foolish to go to war without first sitting down and working out whether you had the possibility of winning, if you could not win you would negotiate a truce.

In the same way we should also count the cost of following Jesus. The cost of which is everything we are and everything we have. If we are not willing to give up everything for Jesus then we should not begin the journey.

It is Biblical to make plans, Habakkuk says, "Write the vision, and make it plain." (Habakkuk 2:2). If there are things that we would really like to do (like my children and a swimming pool) then it is a good and Godly thing to plan, count the cost/ budget, earn and save towards it.

You may want to plan for a special life event. This could be to buy a house, to go on a special holiday or to go to college and gain a qualification. Or you may wish to plan for a child's wedding or their first car or getting them on the property ladder.

It sounds a little harsh to say, but I know that I am saying it to myself as much as anyone else... If you would like to be able to do certain things in the future and you are not planning towards them today then you are more than a little foolish.

As the Proverb says, "Dishonest money dwindles away, but whoever gathers money little by little makes it grow." (Proverbs 11:13).

Hoarding

A lack of planning is not the only foolishness that the Bible warns against. Another is over planning future provision.

Jesus said, 'The ground of a certain rich man yielded an abundant harvest. He thought to himself, 'What shall I do? I have no place to store my crops.' "Then he said, 'This is what I'll do. I will tear down my barns and build bigger ones, and there I will store my surplus grain. And I'll say to myself, "You have plenty of grain laid up for many years. Take life easy; eat, drink and be merry."' But God said to him, 'You fool! This very night your life will be demanded from you. Then who will get what you have prepared for yourself?' This is how it will be with whoever stores up things for themselves but is not rich toward God." (Luke 12:13-21)

It is possible to over plan the future, to store up more than you will ever need for yourself. More commonly we simply call this hoarding. There are trillions of dollars around the world being hoarded in the name of 'reserves' or 'savings' by families, companies and religious organisations. These monies could be put to work through philanthropy, social enterprise or impact investing to alleviate and solve all the poverty on earth.

Jesus also tells this story of… "A certain ruler asked him, 'Good teacher, what must I do to inherit eternal life?' 'Why do you call me good?' Jesus answered. 'No one is good… except God alone. You know the commandments: You shall not commit adultery, you shall not murder, you shall not steal, you shall not give false testimony, honor your father and mother. 'All these I have kept since I was a boy,' he said. When Jesus heard this, he said to him, "You still lack one thing. Sell everything you have and give to the poor, and you will have treasure in heaven. Then come, follow me.' When he heard this, he became very sad, because he was very wealthy. Jesus looked at him and said, 'How hard it is for the rich to enter the kingdom of God! Indeed, it is easier for a camel to go through the eye of a needle than for someone who is rich to enter the kingdom of God.' Those who heard this asked, 'Who then can be saved?' Jesus replied, 'What is impossible with man is possible with God.' Peter said to him, 'We have left all we had to follow you!' 'Truly I tell you," Jesus said to them, 'no one who has left home or wife or brothers or sisters or parents or children for the sake of the kingdom of God will fail to receive many times as much in this age, and in the age to come eternal life." (Luke 18:18-30)

Jesus is not saying that if you are wealthy you have to give up everything in order to follow him. He is saying that if you are not willing to give up anything and everything when asked you cannot follow him. Jesus knew that for this young man his wealth was his God and that in order to follow him he had to give it up but sadly the man would not.

So what is the difference between planning and hoarding? It is like the age old question, 'how much is enough?' There is no universal answer. In any instance it is what Jesus asks you to do. Jesus explains there are future rewards for those who are faithful to him now.

Retirement

When it comes to planning for the future 'retirement' is often something on peoples minds and in their savings plan. I always have to remind myself that, like the thought of being a 'teenager', being 'retired' is not a Biblical concept but a modern sociological construct. That's not to say don't retire but there is no justification in the Bible for retiring from God's calling and living your life in service to him. It makes sense that later in life your body might want you to begin to slow down. The only reason I can think you would want to retire is if you don't like work.

The thought of stopping work and living life on the golf course, at the country club or sailing a boat and waiting to die is really rather tame compared to the life in all its fullness that Jesus calls us to. God does not finish with us when we are finished in full-time employment or enterprise.

I believe in building a life that minimises the difference between work and retirement. Whether we are in full-time paid employment or living off savings, we can live in a place of financial freedom where we are free to pursue Jesus, calling on our life.

Inheritance

Another aspect of financial planning is our financial legacy and the inheritance that others will gain from our hard work. Biblical wisdom says that, "A good person leaves an inheritance for their children's children, but a sinner's wealth is stored up for the righteous." (Proverbs 13:22). So leaving an inheritance to our children and their children's children is a good and Godly thing.

Sir Peter Vardy sold his Reg Vardy car dealerships in 2005 for in excess of $500 million. I have heard him talk publicly about giving significant amounts of that wealth to his three children at that time. One set up a property business, another new car dealerships and the other asked him for help to invest the money. He explained that he believed that his children were ready for wealth and he is around to help them make wise decisions.

The Bible also has another perspective, "An inheritance claimed too soon will not be blessed at the end." (Proverbs 20:21). It is possible that an inheritance can be left to children who are not ready for it and so it can spoil them. The business entrepreneur Andrew Carnegie said, "I would as soon leave to my son a curse as the almighty dollar." All too often large inheritances and trust funds can ruin children robbing them of the necessity to earn a living or else live in poverty.

Sir John Laing (1879–1978) the business entrepreneur and founder of the Laing Construction Group was renowned for his generosity. In 1922 he put almost 40% of his shares in his business into a grant making charitable foundation. He left very little money to his family but set up grant making charities in the names of his wife who died before him and each of his children.

As with many money matters there are few absolutes about inheritance. Some people want to give all their wealth to charity, others want to help their children manage it well and others want to give their children enough to set them up in life but not enough to spoil them. A contemporary Amercian proverb says, 'Wisdom first, wealth second', meaning that a parent should first teach their children to be wise and only then should they be entrusted with wealth.

Life and Financial Priorities

One of the ways I have found it helpful to think about my own life-planning and therefore the financial planning that goes alongside it is to walk through the following process.

I start by asking myself three questions: What would I like to be? What would I like to do? What would I like to have? I brainstorm as many things as I possibly can under each of these three questions. Once I've exhausted everything that I can think of I re-list the items under each of the questions according to their importance to me, also indicating desired timescales. This creates a set of timely priorities against which I can begin to calculate the associated costs of those items and create a plan for saving towards them.

Chuck Bentley, the President of Crown Financial Ministries, kindly reviewed this book before publication and contributed a foreword challenged me to add a fourth question. Chuck suggested asking, "How would I like to be remembered?' which is a powerful probation to consider long-term legacy.

One of the priorities we have chosen as a family is to go on international adventures. I want our children to be confident about travelling, to be internationally minded and to have memories together as a family that they would never forget. Over recent years our travels have included the golden triangle in India seeing the Taj Mahal and forts, a safari in South Africa to see the 'big five' and a California road trip taking in Yosemite National Park. So this is something that we plan for financially.

One of the things I would like to have is a particular sort of car to drive. However, whenever I go through this exercise I decide that family adventures are a greater priority than driving around in the car I would like. Besides that it's easier to go on the underground train into central London, get an Uber home when I've had a late night in town and get a local taxi firm to take me to the airport. So I'm not sure when I would actually drive the car I would like. As Chuck Bentley says, this is financial discipline, you are saying 'no' to what you want today so that you can say 'yes' to what you want tomorrow.

Most of us can't be, do and have everything we would like so we have to make choices between our priorities and plan for our future accordingly.

FREEDOM STEP 9

The ninth step to financial freedom is to plan for the future by counting the cost and taking action now to ensure you can achieve your desires. A significant part of financial freedom is planning ahead to foresee what you will need when.

Brainstorm all things you would like to be, do, have and be remembered for (use a journal if you run out of space).

A) I would like to be ....

....

....

....

....

I would like to do ....

....

....

....

....

I would like to have ....

....

....

....

....

I would like to be remembered for ....

....

....

....

....

B) Define the top three things you want to be, do, have and be remember for and specify their financial cost.

I would like to be:

1] ....

2] ....

3] ....

I would like to do:

1] ....

2] ....

3] ....

I would like to have:

1] ....

2] ....

3] ....

I would like to be remembered for:

1] ....

2] ....

3] ....

C) Name the three you would most like to achieve:

1] ....

2] ....

3] ....

D) Write down your financial plan for achieving these top three goals:

....

....

....

....

....

Step 10:
Use your resources to solve poverty

"Now on his way to Jerusalem, Jesus travelled along the border between Samaria and Galilee. As he was going into a village, ten men who had leprosy met him. They stood at a distance and called out in a loud voice, 'Jesus, Master, have pity on us!' When he saw them, he said, 'Go, show yourselves to the priests.' And as they went, they were cleansed. One of them, when he saw he was healed, came back, praising God in a loud voice. He threw himself at Jesus' feet and thanked him---and he was a Samaritan. Jesus asked, 'Were not all ten cleansed? Where are the other nine? Has no one returned to give praise to God except this foreigner?' Then he said to him, 'Rise and go; your faith has made you well.'"

Luke 17:11-19

A business friend in South Africa has a vision for the construction of an iconic tower in the downtown area of the city of Durban. When he showed me the plans and pictures of what the tower would look like I posted a picture on my social media platforms.

A good friend wrote a provocative comment, "All the poor people will be able to see it from their townships." As much as I love that particular friend I think they missed the point about the positive impact the tower would have upon the city.

The benefits to the city and particularly the poor would be extensive. Such a venture would attract significant domestic and foreign investment. It would create thousands of jobs during the build phase and hundreds more jobs to service the build when finished. It would attract global corporates, national businesses and small/medium sized enterprises creating more jobs and contracts. In short the positive economic impact on the city would be transformational.

There are many approaches to solving poverty and transforming communities and not just through non-profit goodwill or state intervention but also through entrepreneurial business.

Community Transformation

At the time of Jesus, lepers were declared as being 'unclean'. They would then be forced to live in ghettos outside of their village, town or city so they did not contaminate other people. This is why the lepers stood at a distance from Jesus and had to shout in a loud voice in order to be heard by him.

Jesus told the ten lepers to present themselves to the religious leaders of the day because they were responsible for declaring people 'unclean'. The Bible tells us that as the lepers went they were cleansed from their leprosy.

Interestingly only one former leper came back to thank Jesus. You can hardly blame the other nine, they had probably been separated from their wives and children for many years and once they were cleansed all they wanted to do was to run back into their arms.

It does remind us that what we do in the community should be motivated by sacrificial love with no strings attached. The people that we serve and help in the community may not say thank you as a result. They may not come to faith in Christ or come to church.

If we only do what we do in the community in order to get thanked or to get people to come to Christ and come to church then we are not loving sacrificially. We are not loving them as Jesus loves us. Jesus' love is unconditional, he loved us enough to die for us before we ever gave our lives to him. In fact he continues to love us unconditionally and forgive us the many mistakes we make. There are no strings attached to Jesus' love.

It is also worth noting that this was not just a single leper whose life was transformed, instead Jesus transformed a community of ten lepers. It is not clear whether the ten lepers were the entire leper colony or if they were just those who turned up to see Jesus. Whichever, this was an act of community transformation where ten lives were collectively transformed.

Social Inclusion

Jesus transformed the community of lepers by socially including them. They could now leave their ghetto where they had been ostracised and return to normal village life. They could once again live with their families, socialise amongst their friends and enjoy village life.

The Bible points out that the leper that returned to say thank you was a Samaritan and 'foreigner'. This infers that the other nine were probably Jews. This was significant because the Jews are the chosen people of God. The prophet Isaiah says, "I will also make you a light for the Gentiles, that my salvation may reach to the ends of the earth," (Isaiah 49:6b) and yet the Samaritans had been enemies for generations. So as a Jew himself Jesus was showing great generosity. He was also making a statement that the Kingdom of God that he had come declaring and demonstrating was not exclusively for Jews but inclusive for people of every race.

It is hardly surprising that nine of the ten lepers that were healed didn't return to thank Jesus. The men had been separated from their wives and children for years and whilst they would undoubtedly be thankful to Jesus for cleansing them they had other priorities. As soon as the priest declared them clean I can imagine them running into the village shouting that they were healed and running into the arms of their wives and children.

Sadly there are many people in our communities who feel socially excluded and separated from the rest of society, for example elderly people. In the UK, 500,000 elderly people spend Christmas day alone every year and those elderly people living in care homes have on average two minutes of social interaction per day. There are many other groups of people who feel socially excluded such as young people who are excluded from school, minority communities who are victims of prejudice and ex-offenders who find it very difficult to start afresh.

As part of my giving back I founded Cinnamon International a non-profit organisation that is passionate about seeing communities, cities and nations transformed by the life and love of Jesus. We work with national leaders to build networks across their country to catalyse the church in Jesus-centred community transformation. One of our strategic approaches is to identify the best church-led community projects and support those projects to replicate through multiple churches.

In the UK we have helped 30 church-led community projects to replicate through 3,500 local churches. All of the Cinnamon Recognised Projects are focused on social action and practical help, however, the secret to their success actually lies elsewhere. Every beneficiary that I have ever met has appreciated the practical help offered through these projects, however, what has made the greatest difference? What beneficiaries appreciate even more than the practical help is the person who delivered the practical help and the love and relationship they offered them.

The greatest aspect of poverty isn't a lack of money. There are many people around the world who have very little money but they are amongst the happiest and most contented people you will ever meet. Similarly, wealth does not guarantee happiness, some of the most miserable people you will meet are those with the most money.

One of the greatest aspects of poverty is a poverty of relationships. It's the lack of a parental role model or adult mentor in your life to love you and point you in the right direction. It's the lack of a person who offers you their spare bed or sofa when you lose your job and can't afford the rent. It's the lack of a person who supports you when your marriage breaks up and you have to leave the family home. It's the lack of a person who can support you when your mental health deteriorates and you can't maintain life 'as usual'. Without strong social relationships we have no capacity to bounce back when the world around us begins to fall apart and so things go from bad to worse.

Non-profit organisations are not free. Recruiting, training and co-ordinating volunteers and employing community workers costs money, however, they offer incredible value and 'bang for your buck' compared to other social provision. Not only do volunteers offer economic benefits they can also be far more effective. Volunteers normally offer the gift of their time and expertise within their own community or a neighbouring community where they have powerful local knowledge and relational capital. This local connectedness makes the volunteers far more effective in what they do in the community compared to statutory provision.

Many of the issues of poverty faced by our communities are best addressed by building greater social and relational capital where people can share resources.

Economic Empowerment

Jesus transformed the community of lepers by economically empowering them. While living in the ghetto they would have survived by scavenging for scraps of food left out or thrown away by other people. Now that they were clean and could rejoin their society they were able to go to market and begin to work. They could start making a few trades to build up a small amount of capital with which to start a small business.

Handouts are important. They can momentarily help people at a difficult time, however, hand-ups are far more powerful. As the saying goes if you give a man a fish you feed him for a day but if you teach a man how to fish you feed him for life. Charity handouts do not solve poverty. Africa is a powerful example. Over recent decades billions and billions has been given to Africa in aid and relief by charities and governments alike and yet the continent has not been transformed. The only long-term and sustainable solution to poverty is business and enterprise.

Economic empowerment is also powerful in that it gives people dignity and worth which is something charity or government handouts can never provide. I remember a time in my life when I hadn't had any paid work for six months. I was so demoralised and at rock bottom, receiving help from friends kept me going but it did nothing for my self-esteem. It wasn't until business turned around that my self-confidence and self-esteem returned in any measure.

The apostles Peter and John were going to the temple at the time of prayer. At the entrance to the temple was a man who had been lame from birth begging from passers by. Peter turned to the man and said, "Silver or gold I do not have, but what I do have I give to you. In the name of Jesus Christ of Nazareth, walk." (Acts 3:6). What the man experienced of God was far better than he had ever hoped or imagined. He was completely healed and his days of indignity begging for a living were over. Jesus economically empowered him to go out and earn a living.

The Old Testament prophet Elisha met a women whose husband had died and his creditors were coming to take the widow's two sons as slaves in payment for the debt. Elisha asked the widow what she had in her house and she explained, "Your servant has nothing there at all," she said, "except a small jar of olive oil." Elisha said, "Go around and ask all your neighbours for empty jars. Don't ask for just a few." (2 Kings 4:3-4). Elisha then instructed the woman to fill the empty jars she had collected from the jar she owned. Miraculously her oil jar didn't stop flowing until all the other jars were full. Elisha instructed the widow to sell the jars of oil, pay off her husband's debts and live off of what was left. The widow was economically empowered to earn a living.

Employment and enterprise is perhaps the most powerful way of addressing poverty. I just returned from lunch with an entrepreneur who is chief executive of a rapidly growing international business. The number of his employees are doubling every two years and more than half of the workforce are based in impoverished areas of Eastern Europe. The jobs being created are lifting families out of poverty and growing local and national economies.

Jesus is calling entrepreneurs in his church to start businesses that will create tens of thousands and hundreds of thousands of jobs that economically empower people, families and communities who are currently financially impoverished.

Political Justice

Jesus transformed the community of lepers and added greater political pressure to the government of the day. He was challenging the policy that lepers should be excommunicated and forced to live in ghettos.

If politics is defined as the way we choose to live together then the life and work of Jesus profoundly challenges politics. Everything Jesus said and did challenged the political norms of the day. Why should a women caught in adultery be stoned to death while the man goes free? (John 8:3-11) Why should religious people view themselves as self-righteous and distance themselves from those people they view as undesirable? (Mark 2:17).

It is not only peoples' lives that benefit from transformation it's the systems in which we live that also need challenging and changing. Sometimes there are public policies that need changing and updating. Any organised system of society has a tendency to work for the majority rather than the minority. In developing a common view on a matter it is too easy to overlook minority voices and perspectives.

The apostle Paul wrote to the church at Ephesus and said, "For our struggle is not against flesh and blood, but against the rulers, against the authorities, against the powers of this dark world and against the spiritual forces of evil in the heavenly realms." (Ephesians 6:12). Paul is most definitely talking about evil 'spiritual forces' that can oppress people, however, he also talks about 'rulers' and 'authorities' that can be interpreted as political forces that oppress minority groups.

Politics means ensuring there is a level playing field for the whole of society; it is upholding justice and exposing corruption. As Deuteronomy says, "Do not have two differing weights in your bag – one heavy, one light. Do not have two differing measures in your house – one large, one small. You must have accurate and honest weights and measures, so that you may live long in the land the Lord your God is giving you. For the Lord your God detests anyone who does these things, anyone who deals dishonestly." (Deuteronomy 25:13-16).

Good and Godly politicians can use their power and influence to alleviate and solve poverty. This is exactly what Joseph did in his term as Prime Minister of Egypt. He saved resources during the years of abundance so that during the years of famine the people of Egypt would not starve to death. In fact God's plan was bigger than Egypt. The Bible tells us that all that happened to Joseph was for the saving of many lives including the saving of the lineage of God's chosen people Israel (Genesis 45:5-7).

Jesus' life and work was not about spiritual transformation alone it had social, economic and political intent. Jesus really is good news for the poor. He doesn't just empathise with the poor encouraging them to endure because all will be well in heaven. Jesus transforms lives through spiritual, social, economic and political means.

Remember the Poor

The poor are a gospel priority. Jewish faith and tradition prioritises the poor and optimises this in their care for widows and orphans. The Old Testament is pretty explicit about how widows and orphans should be treated, "Do not take advantage of the widow or the fatherless. If you do and they cry out to me, I will certainly hear their cry. My anger will be aroused, and I will kill you with the sword; your wives will become widows and your children fatherless." (Exodus 22:22-24). Jesus maintained this priority, his manifesto declared, "The Spirit of the Lord is on me, because he has anointed me to proclaim good news to the poor." (Luke 4:18a). The gospel is only good news for the poor if it offers a root out of poverty through economic empowerment. Only middle-class Christianity can afford for the gospel to be about spiritual salvation alone.

Jesus' parable about the sheep and the goats (Matthew 25) explains that we will be evaluated by him according to how we treat those people less fortunate than ourselves. The King in the parable says to those people evaluated positively, "For I was hungry and you gave me something to eat, I was thirsty and you gave me something to drink, I was a stranger and you invited me in, I needed clothes and you clothed me, I was sick and you looked after me, I was in prison and you came to visit me." (versus 35-36). Slightly puzzled they asked, "When?" (versus 37-39). Then the King replied, "Truly I tell you, whatever you did for the least of these brothers and sisters of mine, you did for me." (verse 40). Simply put if we remember the poor we will be judged positively by God.

In the New Testament, as the good news of Jesus spreads beyond Israel there is a debate about whether Jewish circumcision is necessary for non-Jewish believers. The answer is of course no. Paul when writing to the church in the city of Galatia writes, "All they asked was that we should continue to remember the poor, the very thing I had been eager to do all along." (Galatians 2:10). Paul finds it necessary to write this because while Jews have a strong sense of social responsibility for the poor, Gentiles/non-Jews do not, so he exhorts them to continue to remember the poor and so should we today.

Following Jesus is not defined by what we don't do but by what we do do. So it's not what we shouldn't do with money that matters the most, it's what we can do with money. There are opportunities to solve poverty by giving philanthropically to leverage and scale interventions that have been demonstrated to work, to invest in businesses that produce a social return as well as an economic return and build businesses that create jobs and lift people out of poverty. Jesus asks us to use our money and other resources for transformational purposes and to live a generous life in all its fullness with him.

FREEDOM STEP 10

The tenth step to financial freedom is to use your spiritual, social, economic and political resources to solve poverty.

A) Write down the main resources and assets that God has put into your hands.

....

....

....

....

....

B) What aspect of poverty are you most concerned about?

....

....

....

C) What sector of society has God called you to work in – non-profit, business or politics?

....

....

....

D) How could you address the area of poverty you are most animated about through the sector God has called you to, using the resources and assets he has put into your hands?

....

....

....

Conclusion

A religious man in the eighteenth century had a most profound God experience...

"It came, somewhat unexpectedly it would appear, at 8.45 on the evening of 24 May 1738 at a meeting in London of which he has left a definite record in his Journal: In the evening, I went very unwillingly to a Society in Aldersgate where one was reading Luther's preface to the *Epistle to the Romans*. I felt my heart strangely warmed: About a quarter before nine, while he was describing the change that God works in the heart through faith in Christ, I felt my heart strangely warmed. I felt I did trust in Christ, Christ alone, for salvation; and an assurance was given me that he had taken away my sins, even mine, and saved me from the law of sin and death."

The Rev John Wesley began preaching about Jesus Christ all over the UK and later around the world. He wasn't welcome in the Church of England and so he began preaching outdoors and then in what became 'preaching houses'. Wesley saw tens of thousands of people often from very working-class communities respond to the gospel of Jesus Christ.

A key emphasis of Wesley's work was building small groups of believers focused on intense discipleship and accountability to one another. The leaders that grew out of this movement were highly socially engaged and were involved in prison reform and the abolition of slavery. Wesley insisted that the Methodist (called such because of its strong methods and processes) movement was part of the Church of England but after his death the Methodist Church emerged.

Wesley taught that you should, "Earn all you can, save all you can and give all you can." He was a man who lived life for Jesus free from concern about money.

My hope and expectation is that you will action these 10 steps and experience greater financial freedom than you have ever known. I pray that like John Wesley you will be able to live your life for Jesus free from anxiety about money.

About the Author

Matt Bird is an international speaker, author and broadcaster. He has spoken in 30 countries to more than 1 million people and authored 11 books.

Matt is CEO/President of Cinnamon International whose vision is to see communities, cities and nations transformed by the life and love of Jesus. Cinnamon catalyses the church in Jesus-centred transformation through strengthening relationships, replicating best-practice and measuring impact. *The Times* newspaper published a story about Cinnamon and its research with the headline, 'Loving thy neighbour is priceless – it is also worth £3 billion.'

He is also CEO/President of Relationology International that increases business performance and business growth through the power of effective relationships. The media magazine *Campaign* said, "When Malcolm Gladwell sat at his typewriter and wrote the chapter on connectors in *The Tipping Point,* he must have just finished a slap-up lunch with Matt Bird."

Matt lives in Wimbledon, London with his wife Esther and their three children.

A Minute with Matt

Each week Matt Bird publishes a 60 second video in which he speaks about someone he has met and something he has learnt from them about business relationships.

You can sign-up FREE at…
www.relationologyinternational.com/free

Cinnamon International Adventure

Each week Matt Bird publishes a 60 second video about the adventure of catalysing the church in Jesus–centred community transformation.

You can sign-up FREE at…
www.cinnamoninternational.com/free